The Little Book of Pointers

Huw Collingbourne

bitwise books

The Little Book Of Pointers

ISBN: 978-1-913132-03-3

bitwise books is an imprint of **dark neon**

written by
Huw Collingbourne

DOWNLOAD THE SOURCE CODE

All the source code of the examples in this book may be downloaded (free) from the publisher's web site:
http://www.bitwisebooks.com/

Contents

Introduction

What is this Book About?

Before we get started, let me say a bit about who this book is for and what you will get out of it. I'm assuming you already have at least some experience of C programming. This is not a book for beginners. If you are completely new to C, you should study my other book, *The Little Book Of C*, before this book. This book is for more experienced C programmers who need to gain a deeper understanding of using pointers.

Download the Source Code

All the source code shown in this book is available for download. The code can be used with any standard C compiler and it may be edited with any programming editor that supports the C language. For the convenience of Visual Studio users, the source code Zip archive contains code in the form of a single Visual Studio multi-project solution.

However, as this is an advanced level book, I am assuming that you are already programming C and you'll probably already have your own favourite C editor. Just create an empty C project in whatever editor you like, then load the supplied code files from one of my projects.

Download the code from the Bitwise Books web site at:

www.bitwisebooks.com

What is in the Book?

This book is entirely about pointers in C: what pointers are and how to use them. It will explain addresses and indirection, how to allocate memory and how to free it when it is no longer needed, how to use pointer arithmetic and how to use pointers with arrays and array elements.

In the later chapters I explain some of the more mysterious features of pointers and memory. Why a `struct` can sometimes take up more memory than the data it contains and why that can cause problems when allocating memory. How to create linked lists, with single or double links, and how to add and delete list elements from the end of a list or from somewhere in the middle. I'll explain how to use pointers with special list types such as stacks and queues, how to use pointers to functions and how to use an array of function pointers.

Finally I'll look at common problems with pointers: memory leaks, dereferencing null pointers, pointers out of scope, errors to do with casting pointers, and problems when making deep and shallow copies.

If you've ever struggled to understand pointers or to use them effectively and safely in your own programs, this is the book for you. It covers a lot of ground – and, when you first see them, some of the topics may be quite hard to grasp. However, this book will illuminate some of the darker, more difficult, types of pointer operations by taking you through them one step at a time. So when you complete this book you will have a deep and solid understanding of pointers in C.

Making Sense of the Text

In this book, any C source code is written like this:

```
int add(int num1, int num2) {
    num1 = num1 + num2;
    return num1;
}
```

Sometimes when a string is too long to fit onto the width of the page in this book, I split over multiple lines using the \ character like this:

```
printf("Here I am displaying a very long string on \
screen, followed by a carriage return\n");
```

The \ character is valid in C as a way of continuing a string onto the next line. In some cases, the \ character may be shown in the listings in the book even though it is not used in the source code archive. That's simply for the sake of readability. It's up to you whether or not you split long strings over multiple lines in your own code.

Any output that you may expect to see on screen when a program is run is shown like this:

```
The result of that calculation is 24!
```

When there is a sample program to accompany the code, the program name is shown above the code like this:

HelloWorld

```
// program code shown here
```

Explanatory notes (which generally provide some hints or give a more in-depth explanation of some point mentioned in the text) are shown in a box like this:

Important

This is an explanatory note. You can skip it if you like – but if you do so, you may miss something of interest…!

About the Author

Huw Collingbourne has been a programmer for more than 30 years. He is an online programming instructor with successful courses on C, C#, Java, Object Pascal, Ruby, JavaScript and other topics. For a full list of available courses be sure to visit the Bitwise Courses web site: http://bitwisecourses.com/

He has written a number of programming books published by Bitwise Books and is the author of *The Book Of Ruby* from No Starch Press. He is a well-known technology writer in the UK and has written numerous opinion and programming columns for a number of computer magazines, such as *Computer Shopper*, *PC Pro*, and *PC Plus*. He is Director Of Technology with SapphireSteel Software.

At various times Huw has been a software developer, magazine publisher, editor, and TV broadcaster. He has an MA in English from the University of Cambridge and holds a 2nd dan black belt in aikido, a martial art which he teaches in North Devon, UK. The aikido comes in useful when trying to keep his Pyrenean Mountain Dogs under some semblance of control.

About the Technical Editor

Dr. Dermot Hogan is a software developer who has led major projects written in Assembly Language, C , C# and a number of other programming languages. A specialist in realtime trading technologies, he has managed and developed global risk management systems for several international banks and financial institutions. Dermot holds a Ph.D in physics from the University of Cambridge. He is the lead developer at SapphireSteel Software. His current area of research is devoted to robotic control and imaging systems.

1 – Introduction to Pointers

If you've ever read a programming book that explains pointers, there's a good chance you've come across diagrams that look something like this…

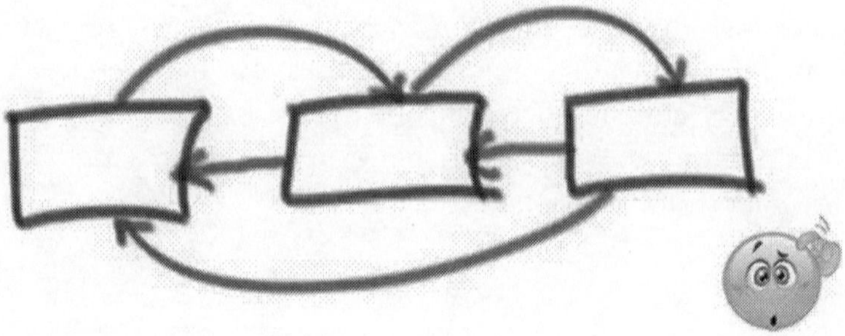

Diagrams like this provide a simplified visual guide to the relationships between pointers and the things they point to. But they don't tell you what a pointer actually *is*. That's what this book is all about.

Pointers and C

In many programming languages, such as Java, Ruby, C# and others, you will either never come across pointers at all or only in very special circumstances. Behind the scenes, all those languages *use* pointers but they hide them from the programmer. That's because pointers can be quite hard to understand and if you use them incorrectly they can cause catastrophic errors.

In C, on the other hand, you can't get away from pointers. That's because C operates at a relatively low level. By 'low level' I mean that it is a language that makes it fairly easy to access the operating system and the computer hardware. This gives C programmers the ability to optimize programs to make them very fast and very efficient. But it also means that C does not protect your programs from making silly, or even dangerous, mistakes. And one of the commonest causes of programmer errors in C are pointers.

What is a Pointer?

Put simply, a pointer is a number. Or, at any rate, the *value* of a pointer variable is a number. That number is the address of a location or 'position' in your computer's memory.

What is an Address?

You can think of computer memory as being a long series of places where data can be stored, just like a very long road full of empty warehouses. Each warehouse has an address (its number) and it may contain something (its data). In computing terms, an address is just a location in memory. A pointer variable stores an address so that we can locate the address, and the data stored there, quickly.

Pointer Variables

Let's see how we can create and use a pointer variable in C:

PointerBasics

```
#include <stdio.h>

int main(int argc, char **argv) {
    int num;
    int* numPtr;
    int num2;

    num = 100;
    numPtr = &num;
    num2 = *numPtr;
    printf("num=%d, numPtr=%d, address of num=%d, num2=%d\n",
            num, numPtr, &num, num2);
    return 0;
}
```

Here I've declared a simple `int` variable called `num` and a pointer variable called `numPtr`. The asterisk or star operator '*' shows that `numPtr` is a pointer and the data type `int` shows that it will point to a memory location containing an integer.

Pointer Declarations

In C, you declare a pointer variable like this:

```
<DataType> * <PointerVariable>
```

Here *<DataType>* can be any valid C data type such as `int`, `char` or user-defined data types. The asterisk or 'star' `*` must come between *<DataType>* and *<PointerVariable>*. This is how to declare a pointer variable called `numPtr` that points to an `int`:

```
int *numPtr;
```

The precise position of the 'star' `*` is unimportant. Some programmers like to place it directly after the type like this `int*`, some prefer to put it directly before the variable like this `*numPtr` and some like to place it between the type and the variable like this: `int * intPtr`. In this book, we adopt the convention of placing the * directly before the variable.

In my short program, I assign an integer value, 100, to my `int` variable `num`. And I set the pointer variable, `numPtr`, to point to the `num` variable. I do that using the 'address-of' operator, the ampersand `&`, in front of the `num` variable. That gets the address – the memory location – of the `num` variable and it assigns that address to the `numPtr` variable:

```
num = 100;
numPtr = &num;
```

Let's be clear on this: the address-of operator '`&`' does *not* return the *value* of the `num` variable, that is 100. It returns the *address* in memory at which that value is stored. That address is now the value of the `numPtr` pointer.

But, of course, just having an address of a variable is not likely to be all that useful unless we can also find out what data is stored at that address. To do that, we need to 'dereference' the pointer.

Dereferencing

Dereferencing means "getting at the data that is pointed to". A pointer provides a reference to an address. When you want to obtain the data at that address itself, you are said to *dereference* the pointer.

Indirection

Let's see how I can find the value of the integer to which my pointer is pointing. The `int` variable, `num2`, does that:

```
num2 = *numPtr;
```

I want to assign to `num2` the *data* stored at the address referenced by pointer variable, `numPtr`. Remember `numPtr` points to the address of the `num` variable (`&num`), and that variable has the value 100.

Here I once again use star operator `*`. When I put a `*` in front of a pointer variable, it returns not the *address*, but the *data* that is found at that address. So *without* the star `numPtr` returns the pointer's *value* (the address of `num`), but *with* the star `*numPtr` returns the *contents* of that address – that is, the integer 100 – and that is how I have been able to assign 100 to the `int` variable `num2` in the code shown above.

This final line of code in the *PointerBasics* program:

```
printf("num=%d, numPtr=%d, address of num=%d, num2=%d\n",num,numPtr,&num,num2);
```

This prints the *values* of `num` and of `numPtr`, the *address* of `num` and the *value* of `num2`. When I run this program, this is what I see:

```
num=100, numPtr=13629500, address of num=13629500, num2=100
```

So here you can see that the value of `num` variable is, as expected, 100. But the value of the pointer variable, `numPtr` is 13629500 which is the *address* of the `num` variable. I can verify that by using 'address-of' operator `&` to display the address of the `num` variable, `&num`, which shows the same number: 13629500. You will almost certainly see a different number when you run the code because it is extremely unlikely that the program will store the data at exactly the same address in memory on your computer as on mine.

In fact, if you run the program several times, you may see different addresses. The addresses are not fixed when you compile your program. They are allocated when the program is run using whichever memory locations are available at that time.

%p or %d?

It is generally considered that the 'correct' way to display pointer values or addresses in formatted strings is to use `%p` to show a hexadecimal value. However, in my examples I sometimes use `%d` to show decimal values. I do that because most people understand decimal values more easily than hexadecimal values.

This becomes more important later in the book when we need to see how many bytes separate one address from another. For example, look at these two hexadecimal values which represent memory addresses: `006FFE18, 006FFE2C`. Unless you are very familiar with hexadecimal, it may not be obvious exactly how many bytes separate the second address from the first address.

Now look at these two decimal values which are exact equivalents of the hexadecimal values: `7339544, 7339564`. It should be immediately clear that the second number is 20 greater than the first number. As these are addresses, we can see that the second address is separated by 20 bytes from the first address. When it is not important to count the bytes in this way, I may show the more conventional hexadecimal values.

2 – Addresses and Arrays

The address of an array is the same as the address of the first item in that array. Why is this important? In order to understand that, you need to be sure that you understand what an array actually is.

In many programming languages, arrays are treated as high-level structures: lists of elements than can be accessed using an index. In C, that definition isn't good enough. To use arrays safely, you have to understand how arrays are actually stored in computer memory. And that all begins with the address of the array.

Arrays

The address of the array is the same as the address of the first element in the array because that is the address where the array begins. The name of the array – that is the name you give to the array identifier – is also the address of the array. To explain this, let's look at how strings are used in C.

Strings

C does not have a dedicated string data type. In C, a string is just an array of characters. For convenience, C treats the null character `'\0'` as the string terminator. When you declare a string like this, C automatically adds a null character at the end:

```
char str1[] = "Hello world";
```

Let's see if we can find where this string is stored in memory. Here's my program:

StringsAndPointers

```
#include <stdio.h>

int main(int argc, char **argv) {
    char str1[] = "Hello world";

    printf("%s %c %d %d %d\n", str1, str1[0], &str1, &str1[0], str1);
    return 0;
}
```

And this is the output:

```
Hello world H 17825380 17825380 17825380
```

This displays the string `"Hello world"` which is the array of characters assigned to the identifier `str1`. Then it shows the character at index 0, `str1[0]`, which here is the 'H' of `"Hello world"`. Then it prints the address of the array, `&str1`, which is this number (here `17825380`) representing the memory location of the character array `str1`. Then it prints the address of the first character in the character array, `&str1[0]`, which is the same (`17825380`) as the address of the array itself. And finally it prints `str1` as an integer (using `%d`) instead of as a string (using `%s`) and once again the address of the array is shown (`17825380`).

%s or %d

Why does `%d` display the address of the string but `%s` displays the string itself? When displaying a string using a numeric format specifier such as `%d` or `%p`, the `printf()` function displays the address of the start of the array. But when displaying a string using the string format specifier `%s` it reads and shows all the characters starting at the address of the string identifier (the first character in the array of characters) up until the first null character which terminates the string.

Let me repeat what I said at the beginning of this chapter, because it is important that you understand this:

- The address of an array is the same as the address of the first item in the array.
- The name of the array – that is the name you give to the array identifier – is also the address of the array.

In other words, while we may tend to think of arrays as fixed-length lists, in fact, an array is really an address. It is the address at which the first element in a list of data elements is stored.

When we iterate over the elements in an array, we are really moving to new addresses at offsets from the start of the array. An offset is a certain number of bytes (the number of bytes depends on the size of each data element) away from the starting address of the array.

In other programming languages, you may not need to understand the nitty-gritty details of arrays and addresses. In C, you do. Often when you are dealing with arrays you will be using pointers. That's because arrays are addresses. And pointers are what we use when accessing addresses.

Arrays, Addresses and Pointers

Let's look more closely at how pointers and addresses work – and why arrays are special.

ArraysAndAddresses

```
#include <stdio.h>

int main(int argc, char **argv) {
    char str1[] = "Hello";
    char *str2 = "Goodbye";
    printf("%d %d %s\n", &str1, str1, str1);
    printf("%d %d %s\n", &str2, str2, str2);
    return 0;
}
```

Here I declare two strings, `str1` and `str2`. You can create strings using either syntax (`char str1[]` or `char *str1`) but you need to understand that these two declarations are by no means the same as one another.

The first, `str1`, declared with a pair of square brackets, is an array. The second, `str2`, declared using the star operator * is a pointer, and so it's a variable. As we know, an array and an address are equivalent. So `str1` is the address at which the array of characters in the string `"Hello"` are stored. But `str2` is a pointer whose value is the address of the string `"Goodbye"`.

In fact, `str1` isn't a variable because its value (the address of an array) cannot be changed. The *contents* of the array – its individual elements – can be changed. The address of the array, however, cannot. That is why I prefer to call `str1` an array 'identifier', though many people would call it, somewhat inaccurately, an 'array variable'.

When I run the *ArraysAndAddresses* program, these two `printf()` statements are run:

```
printf("%d %d %s\n", &str1, str1, str1);
printf("%d %d %s\n", &str2, str2, str2);
```

And this is what is displayed:

```
7339688 7339688 Hello
7339676 13794104 Goodbye
```

Is an array a pointer?

If the value of an array identifier such as `char str1[]` and the value of a pointer variable such as `char *str2` are both addresses, aren't `str1` and `str2` both pointers?

No, they are not.

Many programming books and tutorials state that array identifiers are 'pointer variables'. This is incorrect. It is an essential feature of a variable that its value can be changed. The value of an array identifier cannot be changed.

What's more, a pointer variable occupies one address; its value can be set to point to different addresses. But an array identifier and its address are one and the same thing.

How can that be?

You have to understand what happens during compilation. When your program is compiled, the array identifier, `str1`, is *replaced* by the address of the array. That address cannot be changed when your program is run. But `str2` is a pointer variable with its own address. Its value (the address of an array) can change if new addresses are assigned to the pointer variable.

char str1[ ]

Look carefully at the first line of the output shown above – when `&str1` and `str1` are displayed as integer values. Notice that the *address* of the character array `&str1` (returned by the address-of operator `&`) is the *same* as the *value* of the identifier `str1` itself (`7339688`). That's because `str1` is an array and an array is, in effect, an address.

char *str2

But, in the second line of output, you see that the *address* of `&str2` (`7339676`) is *different* from the *value* of the `str2` variable (`13794104`). Here `&str2` gives us the location in memory of the pointer variable, `str2`. But the *value* of that variable (`str2`) is the address of the array of chars to which it points.

Think back to the analogy I gave earlier on. I need to find a warehouse on a road containing many warehouses. I have a card on which is written the address of a specific warehouse – "Warehouse 13". That card is like a pointer variable. It is not the actual physical location of the warehouse. It is a reference to that location. The card stores a value that lets me find the location of the warehouse.

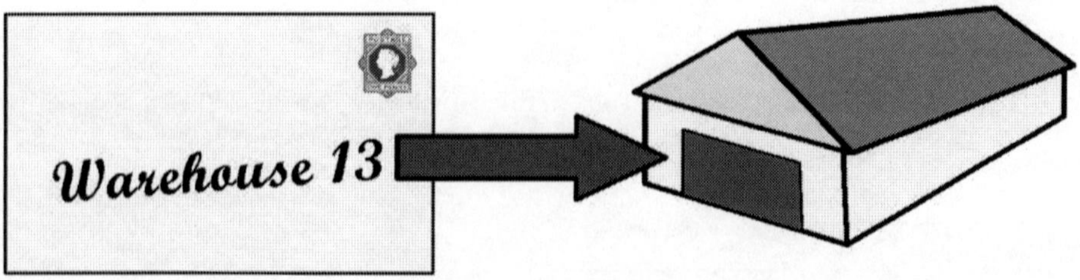

That is, in effect, what a pointer variable does. An array, just like a warehouse, occupies a physical location. A pointer variable, like the card, stores the address of that location.

str1[] and *str2

In summary, look at the code in two the `printf()` statements again and compare it with the output. You can see that `&str1`, and `str1` are identical – they are both the address of the character array `"Hello"`. But `&str2` and `str2` are different things. `&str2` is the *address of the pointer variable* whereas `str2` is the *value of the pointer variable*: and that *value* happens to be the *address of the character array* `"Goodbye"`.

Array Initialization

Look at this short, example. In this case, I want both to declare and initialize an array:

```
int p1[] = {1,2,3};
```

Compare the code above with code shown below:

```
int *p2 = {1,2,3};
```

The first example will compile, while the second will not. Why is this?

The first example (`int p1[]`) declares `p1` as an *array* – that's what the square brackets mean. So it can take an array initializer (`{1,2,3}`) – that's what the curly brackets do.

The second example (`int *p2`) declares `p2` as a *pointer* and tries to initialize it with the *address* of the array initializer in curly brackets. C syntax does not allow this, so it fails.

Visualizing Pointers and Arrays

To help clarify the relationship between an array, an address and a pointer, look at this diagram:

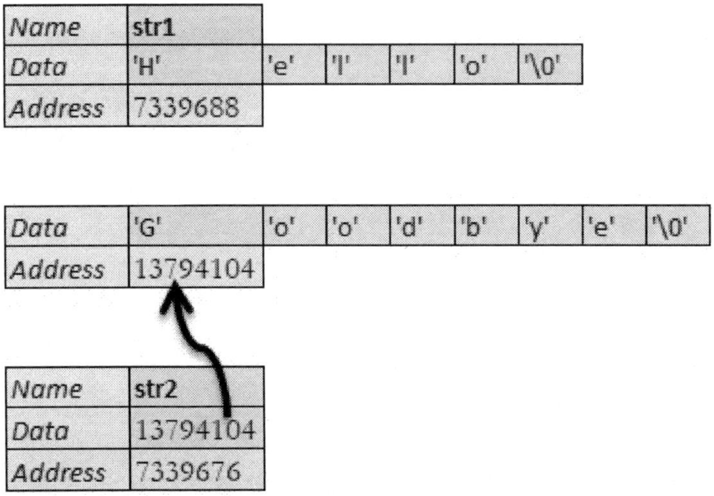

The diagram shows an array of `char`, `str1`, and a pointer to `char`, `str2`. I might create those using this code:

```
char str1[] = "Hello";
char *str2 = "Goodbye";
```

`str1` is the address of the character array `"Hello"` and it is also the address of the first char `'H'` in that array: `7339688`.

`str2` (the pointer) has its *own* address (`7339676`) but its *value* – the data that the pointer 'contains' – is a *different* address (`13794104`) which is the address of the `char` array `"Goodbye"` and also of the first character `'G'` in that array.

In this example, the array `"Goodbye"` does not have a name. It simply exists as some characters stored at an address. The only way to get at those characters is by using the pointer, `str2`, to find the location of the array of characters.

Assigning an Address to a Pointer

If you still find this confusing, try playing around with the code in the sample program *ArraysAndAddresses*. For example, try this simple experiment. Assign the array `str1`, `"Hello"` (which is an address), to the pointer variable `str2`:

ArraysAndAddresses

```
str2 = str1;
```

When you run the program, this is what you'll see:

```
1125120548 1125120548 Hello
1125120584 1125120548 Hello
```

Now, assign the *address* of the array `str1` to `str2`:

```
str2 = &str1;
```

Run the program again, and you will see something very striking about the output: `str1` and `&str1` are equivalent. While, of course, the actual addresses will no doubt be different from the ones I see (and, in fact, the addresses also change when I rebuild and run the program), the important thing to note is that whether I specify `str1` or `&str1` I end up assigning the *address* of `str1`. And the *value* of the pointer `str2` is set to the *address* of the array `"Hello"`.

```
11992276 11992276 Hello
11992264 11992276 Hello
```

Now it is quite possible that your compiler will object to assigning the address using the `&` operator as in the example above and it may show you a warning. The point here is not to encourage you to assign `&str` in this way but to show you that the array `str1` and the *address* of `str1` are one and the same thing.

3 – Indirection

I mentioned indirection in Chapter 1. 'Indirection' is the term used to describe the process of using a pointer to access the data stored at an address. The term 'dereferencing' is also used to describe this.

You may recall that the indirection operator is the 'star' `*`. In the code fragment that follows, I use the indirection operator to obtain the value of the integer to which the `numPtr` pointer is pointing. I then assign that value to the `int` variable, `num`:

```
num = *numPtr;
```

Often in C you may want to use a pointer to access data to which some *other* pointer is pointing. When you follow a trail that leads from one pointer to another pointer (or even to several other pointers) in order to get at some data, we call this 'multiple indirection'.

Multiple Indirection

Let's suppose you have a pointer variable called `pi` which points to an integer. You have another pointer variable, called `ppi` that points to the pointer variable, `pi`. When I declare `pi` as a pointer to an integer I write this:

```
int *pi;
```

But when I declare `ppi`, as a pointer to a pointer to an integer, I have to use two indirection operators to show that this is a *pointer-to-a-pointer* like this:

```
int **ppi;
```

You may wonder why on earth you'd want to do that. Well, multiple indirection can be used when working with lists and arrays. You might have lists of lists that are accessed using pointers to pointers. We'll see examples of this sort of thing later in this book. Don't worry about that for now, though. At the moment, all you need to know is how pointers to pointers actually work. Even if you don't use these in your own programs, you need to be able to understand them if you see them in other people's programs.

Multiple Indirection with Integers

Let's start by looking at a fairly simple example of multiple indirection. Here I declare an array to store three integers:

MultipleIndirection

```
#define LENGTH 3
int data[LENGTH];
```

This loop puts the integers 0, 1 and 2 into the `data` array:

```
for (int i = 0; i < LENGTH; i++) {
    data[i] = i;
}
```

And *this* loop prints those values for me to check that everything is correct:

```
for (int i = 0; i < LENGTH; i++) {
    printf("%d\n", data[i]);
}
```

Levels of Indirection

Let's see how to access those values using both *simple* indirection – that is, using a pointer to an integer – and *multiple* indirection: using a pointer to a *pointer* to an integer. I warn you in advance that, even though this is a very short program, you may need to stare at this code quite a while in order to understand what's going on.

As shown in the preceding code fragments, I begin by creating an array called `data`, containing three integers, 0, 1, 2 (here its address in hexadecimal is `009CA480`):

data	0	1	2
009CA480			

I declare two pointer variables: `pi` which is a pointer to an `int`. And `ppi` which, as it is declared with two asterisks, is a pointer to a *pointer* to an `int`:

```
int *pi;
int **ppi;
```

As we know, an array is an address. So I can simply assign the address of the `data` array (which is the same as the address of the array's first element, here the integer 0), to my pointer variable `pi`:

```
pi = data;
```

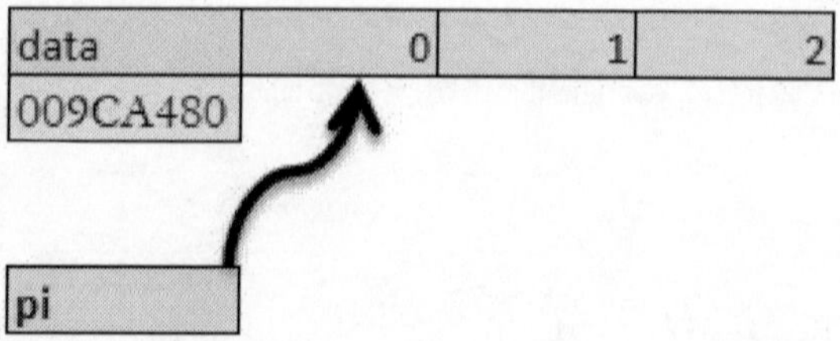

So now `pi` points to the address of the `data` array (or the first element of that array).

I then assign the address of the pointer variable `pi` using the `&` address-of operator to my pointer-to-pointer variable `ppi`:

```
ppi = &pi;
```

So now:

- `pi` is a pointer which points to the `data` array.
- `ppi` points to the pointer, `pi`.

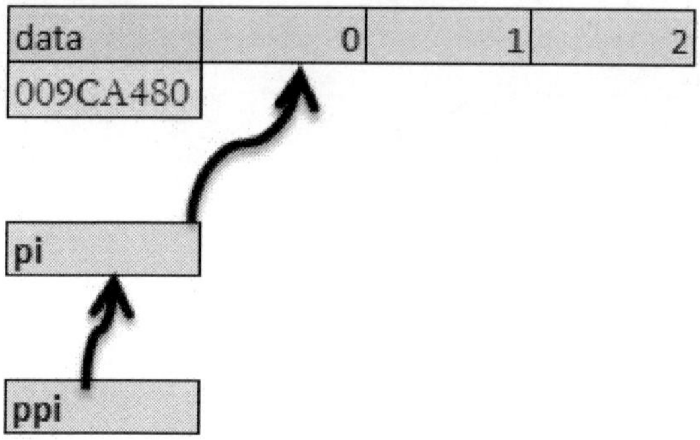

The `for` loop shown below iterates over all the elements of this three-element array – from the element at index 0 to the element at index 2. And it prints out various bits of information which we'll look at shortly:

```
for (int i = 0; i < LENGTH; i++) {
    printf("array address is %p\n", data);
    printf("item pointed to by pi is %d\n", *pi);
    printf("item pointed to by ppi is %p\n", *ppi);
    printf("item pointed to by double indirection of ppi is %d\n\n", **ppi);
    printf("The address of pi is %p and the value of ppi (what it points to) is \
%p\n\n", &pi, ppi);
    pi += 1;
}
```

At each turn through the loop, 1 is added to the pointer variable, `pi`:

```
pi += 1;
```

Each time I add 1 to `pi`, you can think of `pi` as being advanced by one element – so that it points to the next element in the array:

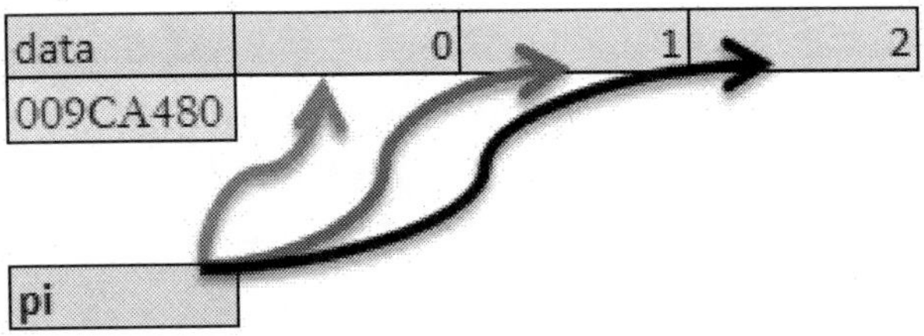

This is a simple example of pointer arithmetic which will be explained later in this book. Now let's look more closely at these `printf()` statements.

The first `printf()` prints address of the `data` array. Here I have stuck to the convention of using the `%p` format specifier which prints an address as a hexadecimal value:

```
printf("array address is %p\n", data);
```

The array address never changes, of course, so the same number is shown at each turn through the loop.

```
array address is 009CA480
array address is 009CA480
array address is 009CA480
```

Next I dereference the `int` pointer `pi`, to display the integer (the actual data that is stored) at each index of the array:

```
printf("item pointed to by pi is %d\n", *pi);
```

One Level of Indirection

At the first turn through the loop, `pi` points to the start of the array so the first element, 0, is shown. In subsequent turns through the loop the other integers in the array, 1 and 2, are shown.

```
item pointed to by pi is 0
item pointed to by pi is 1
item pointed to by pi is 2
```

Two Levels of Indirection

Now I display the item pointed to by `ppi`:

```
printf("item pointed to by ppi is %p\n", *ppi);
```

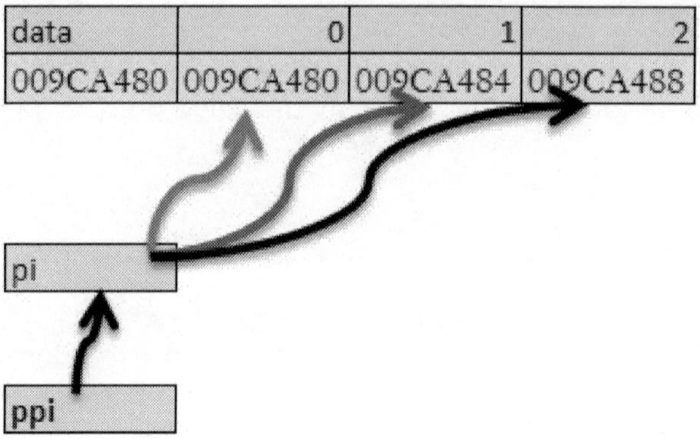

Recall that `ppi` is a pointer that points to another pointer `pi`. I assigned the `data` array to `pi`. At the *first turn* through the loop `ppi` is dereferenced to get the value stored at whatever it points to. It points to the pointer variable `pi` – and the value of `pi` is the address of the `data` array.

```
array address is 009CA480
item pointed to by ppi is 009CA480
```

So we can see that `ppi` points to `pi` – and `pi` points to the `data` array. In order to go further and get the *value* pointed to by the pointer `pi` I need to use this double indirection operator, `**ppi`. This, in effect, says: *get the value of what is pointed to by the pointer that* `ppi` *points to.*

Here `ppi` points to the pointer `pi`; and `pi` points to an `int`. So `**ppi` gets the value of the `int` pointed to by `pi`.

Many levels of indirection!

In C, you aren't restricted to just one or two levels of indirection. It is possible to have pointers to pointers to pointers to pointers if you really want to, like this:

```
int ****ppi;
```

That might be useful in some cases but it would be confusing when learning to use pointers so we will stick to one or two levels of indirection.

Iteration Using Pointer Arithmetic

At each turn through the loop `pi` is incremented to point to the next element of the array (`pi += 1`) and when I use double indirection `**ppi` returns the value pointed to by `pi` – that is, the next integer in the array.

This is my code:

```
printf("item pointed to by ppi is %p\n", *ppi);
printf("item pointed to by double indirection of ppi is %d\n\n", **ppi);
```

And this is what is printed in the three turns through the loop:

```
item pointed to by ppi is 009CA480
item pointed to by double indirection of ppi is 0

item pointed to by ppi is 009CA484
item pointed to by double indirection of ppi is 1

item pointed to by ppi is 009CA488
item pointed to by double indirection of ppi is 2
```

Pointing to the Address of Another Pointer

I know this can be hard to follow so let's look at this final `printf()` statement:

```
printf("The address of pi is %p and the value of ppi (what it points to) \
is %p\n\n", &pi, ppi);
```

This displays the *address* of the pointer variable `pi` and the *value* of the pointer variable `ppi`.

```
The address of pi is 00CFFA78 and the value of ppi (what it points to) is
00CFFA78
```

The two numbers are the same. And they *stay* the same at each turn through the loop. That shows that the value stored by the `ppi` variable is the *address* of the `pi` pointer variable. In this program, that address never changes.

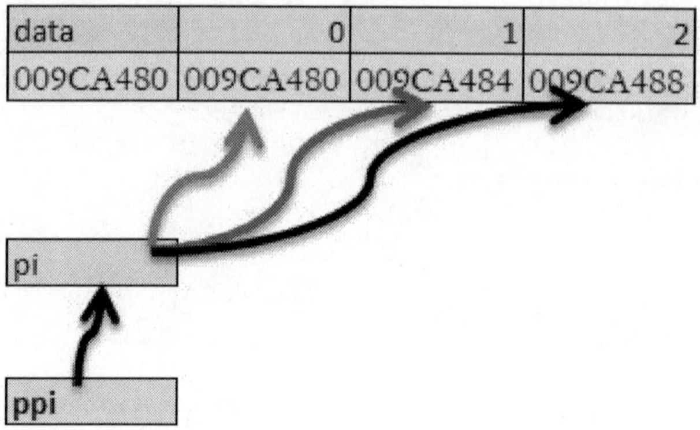

In summary, *one level* of indirection `*ppi` gets the *value* of the pointer `pi` which here happens to be the address of the first integer (0) in the `data` array.

Two levels of indirection `**ppi` gets the element stored at the address that is pointed to by `pi`. In this program that is one of the integers in the `data` array: 0, 1 or 2. Each integer in the array has its own address, as shown in the preceding diagram.

The first element in the array (here the integer 0) has the same address as the array itself. Each subsequent element has an address which is at an 'offset' (a certain number of bytes of memory) from the start of the array. I'll explain this in more detail when we look at pointer arithmetic later on.

Still Confused?

Indirection can be hard to understand at first. *Multiple indirection* is even more difficult. You may need to use a debugger to step through the code in the *MultipleIndirection* sample project, one line at a time. It really is worth the effort. Once you understand this, you will have crossed one of the major barriers to understanding how pointers work.

Multiple Indirection with Strings

Let's look at another example of multiple indirection – this time with an array of strings.

MultipleIndirectionStrings

```
#include <stdio.h>
#define LENGTH 3
char *words[LENGTH];        // some strings

int main(int argc, char **argv) {
    char *pc;               // pointer to a character
    char **ppc;             // pointer to a pointer to a character

    printf("multiple indirection example\n");

    words[0] = "zero";
    words[1] = "one";
    words[2] = "two";
    for (int i = 0; i < LENGTH; i++) {
        printf("%s\n", words[i]);
    }

    ppc = words;
    for (int i = 0; i < LENGTH; i++) {
        ppc = words + i;
        pc = *ppc;
        while (*pc != 0) {
            printf("%c ", *pc);
            pc += 1;
        }
        printf("\n");
    }

    return 0;
}
```

Here I have a `char` pointer, `pc`, and a pointer-to-a-`char`-pointer, `ppc`. I have declared an array, `words`, to hold some strings.

A String Pointer is a Pointer to Char

In C, a string is an array of characters terminated by the null character `'\0'` so I can declare a string as a pointer to a `char` – that is, a pointer to the address of the start of the array of characters in a string.

When I initialize a string or, as here, a string element in an array, C automatically appends a null character to that string:

```
words[0] = "zero";
```

In this example, the string at index 0 of the words array contains these characters: `'z', 'e', 'r', 'o', '\0'`.

So we now have an array named `words` containing three elements. Each element is itself an array of chars (the strings `"zero"`, `"one"`, `"two"`):

words[0]	'z'	'e'	'r'	'o'	'\0'
words[1]	'o'	'n'	'e'	'\0'	
words[2]	't'	'w'	'o'	'\0'	

This code assigns to my `ppc` variable, the address of the words array:

```
ppc = words;
```

In a `for` loop I iterate through the array of strings and in the `while` loop (which is inside the `for` loop), I iterate through the characters in each string:

```
for (int i = 0; i < LENGTH; i++) {
    ppc = words + i;
    pc = *ppc;
    while (*pc != 0) {
        printf("%c ", *pc);
        pc += 1;
    }
    printf("\n");
}
```

The code in the `while` loop prints the characters one by one, with a space between each character. On the first turn through the `for` loop, this is displayed:

```
z e r o
```

Moving Through Strings in the Array

The `for` loop moves the `ppc` pointer through the `words` array, from one element to the next, by adding 1 to the array address:

```
ppc = words + i;
```

When I say it *moves* the pointer, what I mean is that the address – the *number*, stored by the pointer variable – is updated to a different address at each turn through the loop. We can think of this as 'moving' the pointer because the value the pointer variable stores determines the address that can be accessed using the pointer.

In fact, each time 1 is added to `words`, a value that is one "pointer's worth" of memory (which happens to be 4 bytes) is added to the value of the *address* of the `words` array.

This incremented value is assigned to `ppc`. This has the effect of 'moving' `ppc` to point to the address of the next string (that is, a pointer to a `char`) in the array.

On the first turn through the `for` loop, the address of the `words` array is not incremented at all because the initial value of `i` is 0. So `ppc` points to the address of the `words` array and therefore to the first element of that array:

```
for (int i = 0; i < LENGTH; i++) {
    ppc = words + i;
```

In subsequent turns through the `for` loop, `i` has the value 1 and then 2 so when `i` is added to `words`, the `ppc` pointer is moved to the second and third elements (`char` pointers) in the `words` array.

The result is that each string in the array is displayed one character at a time, with each character separated from the next by a space character. This is done by the code in the `while` loop (which we'll look at more closely shortly):

```
z e r o
o n e
t w o
```

The diagram that follows shows what happens as the loop runs three times. The `ppc` pointer initially points to `words[0]`, then to `words[1]` and finally to words`[2]`, where each element is the address of a string. Within the `for` loop, the pointer `pc` is assigned the value or 'contents' of the `ppc` pointer (`*ppc`). That value is the address of one of the strings. So now `pc` also points to the start of each string:

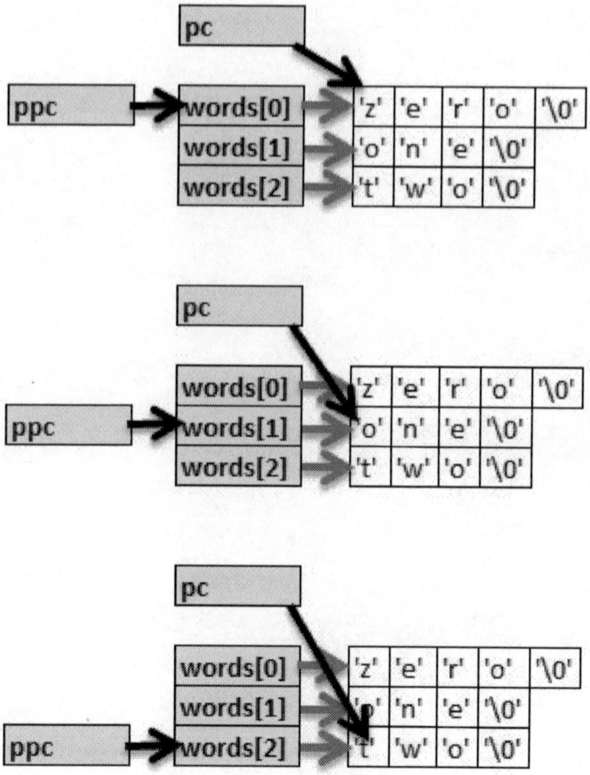

If there were only this single `for` loop in my code, that would be the end of the story. But the `for` loop contains a `while` loop. Let's see what that does next.

Moving Through Chars in Each String

The `while` loop increments `pc` to move through the current string. It does that by incrementing the address of the first `char` in a string and assigning that new address to the `pc` pointer: `pc += 1`. This causes pc to 'move' to the next `char` and the next `char` after that and so on until the terminating null `char` is found. The diagram that follows shows how `pc` is updated to point to the next character in the current string at each turn through the `while` loop.

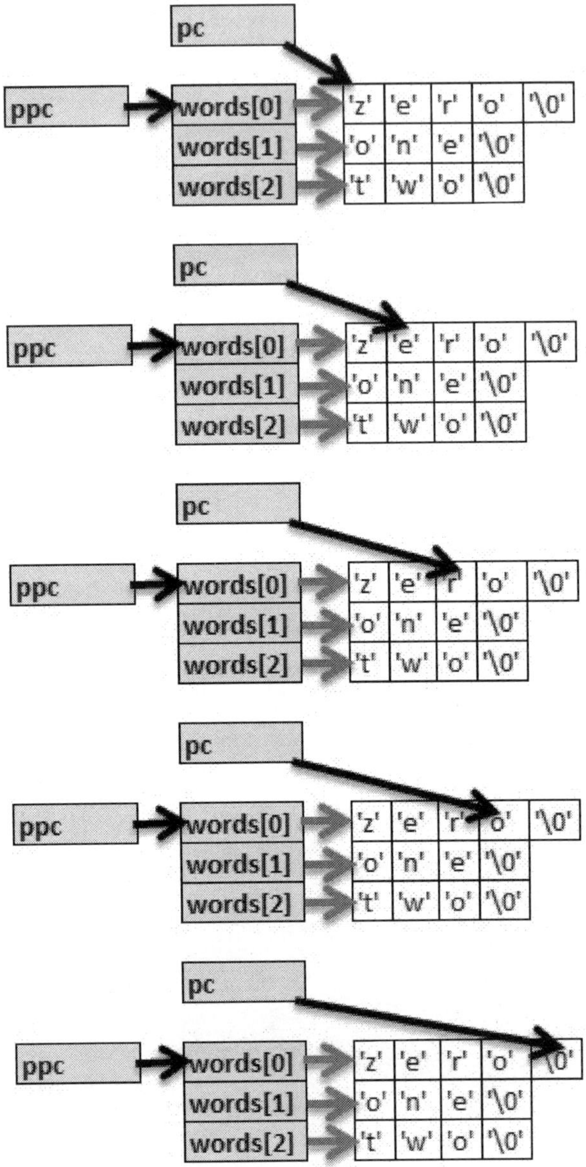

On the first time though the `for` loop, `ppc` would point to the first element (a pointer to `char`) in the `words` array and `pc` would point to the first `char` of the first string.

The value of pc would then be incremented so that it would move through each character in the string (and so on for each other string in the words array):

```
while (*pc != 0) {
    printf("%c ", *pc);
    pc += 1;
}
```

The code dereferences the pointer in order to print the current character. It does that by placing an asterisk (the indirection operator) before it (*pc).

Indirection and Command-line Arguments

Here's another very common example of multiple indirection. This program displays any arguments passed to it on the command line, one argument per line.

CommandLineArgs

```
int main(int argc, char **argv) {
    int i;

    for (int i = 0; i < argc; i++) {
        printf("arg %d is %s\n", i, argv[i]);
    }

    printf("\n\n");

    for (i = 0; i < argc; i++) {
    printf("arg %d is %s\n", i, *argv);
        argv += 1;
    }
    return 0;
}
```

You will often find that the main() function of a C program declares the argument argv preceded by two stars:

```
int main(int argc, char **argv)
```

As you know that means argv is a pointer to a pointer to, in this case, a char. It is initialized with any arguments passed at the command line. The argc argument is an integer which supplies the number or 'count' of arguments.

If you want to access the arguments you can simply treat argv as an array and print out the strings in a simple for loop as I have done here:

```
for (int i = 0; i < argc; i++) {
    printf("arg %d is %s\n", i, argv[i]);
}
```

But you could equally well iterate through the elements by moving the `argv` pointer (`argv += 1`) and then make use of the dereference operator (`*argv`) at each turn through the loop to access the current string:

```
for (i = 0; i < argc; i++) {
    printf("arg %d is %s\n", i, *argv);
    argv += 1;
}
```

You could try this out by building the sample program, *CommandLineArgs*, and passing some arguments to the executable program when you run it from the system prompt. For example, let's suppose you run it by entering this at the command prompt:

```
CommandLineArgs 1 2 three four
```

This would be the result:

```
arg 0 is CommandLineArgs
arg 1 is 1
arg 2 is 2
arg 3 is three
```

The first argument (`arg 0`) is the program name itself and subsequent arguments are any strings entered after the program name.

Generic Pointers

So far we've used pointers to specific data types such as `int` and `char`. But sometimes you may want to write code that can deal with pointers to any type of data. For example, you may want to write some code that can sort data but you don't want to duplicate that code by writing one function to sort characters, another function to sort integers, another for floating points and so on. In that case, you can use generic pointers instead of pointers to predefined data types.

A generic pointer is written as a pointer to `void`. When you use a generic pointer to access some data you must first cast it to a specific data type.

Casts

A 'cast' is an instruction to the compiler to treat compatible types as equivalent. When you cast one type to another type you are, in effect, telling the compiler to stop complaining. A cast is done by placing the intended type between parentheses prior to the variable or expression that returns a value. But be careful. Incorrect casts may cause problems – as we'll see when we look at common pointer problems in Chapter 10.

Let's consider a short example. As in previous examples, I've created an array of integers, data:

GenericPointers

```
int data[LENGTH];
```

But this time, I have declared a generic pointer, gp:

```
void *gp;
```

Having added some integers to the data array, I then assign data (the array address) so that gp points to the start of that array:

```
gp = data;
```

Even though data is typed to hold integers, I don't need to cast the generic pointer here as I am not yet trying to access any actual elements of the array.

I *do* need a cast when I want to refer to one of the integers in the array, however. To do that I have to cast gp to a pointer to int:

```
(int*)gp
```

So gp is a pointer, whose value is now the address of the first integer in the data array. I now need to use the star * dereference operator, before the (int) cast to get the value, the int, at this address:

```
*(int*)gp
```

Now I am able to print the integer pointed to by gp:

```
printf("item pointed to by gp is %d\n", *(int*)gp);
```

The meaning of *

The asterisk ('star') operator has several different meanings in C. We use stars to declare pointer variables like this:

```
void *gp;
char *words[LENGTH];
```

We use a star to cast a generic pointer such as gp to a specific pointer type like this:

```
 (int*)gp
```

And we use a star to dereference pointers (and pointers to pointers) like this:

```
*pi;
*(int*)gp
**ppi;
```

It's easy to be confused by all those stars (and that's not even counting the * multiplication operator: `2 * 5` etc.), so you may need to look very carefully at code containing stars in order to understand its meaning.

Here I add 1 to gp in order to move the pointer to the next array index. I cast gp to a pointer to int, and I can then print the second integer:

```
gp = (int*)gp + 1;
printf("item pointed to by gp is now %d\n", *(int*)gp);
```

But as gp is a *generic* pointer, I should be able to use it not only with integers but with other data types too. As in the previous example, I have once again created a words array:

```
char *words[LENGTH];
```

I've added three strings to this array:

```
words[0] = "zero";
words[1] = "one";
words[2] = "two";
```

Even though I have already cast `gp` to point to an array of integers, I can now point `gp` to the `words` array of strings:

```
gp = words;
```

I need to cast `gp` in order to access one of the strings stored in that array:

```
(char**)gp
```

But why the *two* stars in this cast? Remember that an array of strings is, in effect, an *array of arrays* of characters. So my cast here has to be a *pointer to a pointer* to `char` – that's `char**` between parentheses.

And I use the dereference operator – a single asterisk preceding the parentheses – to access the string when I want to print it:

```
printf("item pointed to by gp is %s\n", *(char**)gp);
```

I iterate to the next index, again casting to `char**`, and I print the second string:

```
gp = (char**)gp + 1;
printf("item pointed to by gp is now %s\n", *(char**)gp);
```

So you can see how, by using a generic pointer, I have been able to access different types of data. In some programs – if for example, the data type may vary and you don't want to write repetitive code for each data type – that could be useful.

4 – Allocating Memory

When I created arrays and strings in the previous examples, I sometimes declared each array or string with a fixed length prior to initializing it:

```
#define LENGTH 3
int data[LENGTH];
```

And sometimes, I assigned a string at the time of its declaration:

```
char str1[] = "Hello world";
```

In both cases, the actual size – that is, the amount of memory – needed to hold the data is known before I run the program so the C compiler is able to set aside the correct amount of memory to store all the data.

But what if I need to create an array at runtime?

Say, for example, the user enters a string at the command prompt or some data is read in from a disk file. I can't know, prior to compiling my code, exactly how much data I'll be dealing with. It might be a string containing two or three characters or it could be text from a file containing tens of thousands of characters.

When I create an array to hold those characters, or other types of data whose actual size may only be known at runtime, I need some way of calculating how much memory I need to store the data.

I then need to allocate that memory – that is, I need to ask the C runtime system to reserve a chunk of memory sufficient hold exactly the right amount of data.

Only by doing that can I be sure that I won't overwrite some memory that's already been allocated for some other data. Memory corruption of this sort is a serious bug and can cause a program to malfunction or crash.

Strings

Let's see how we can handle memory allocation in C. Let's start with a function that receives a string as an argument and returns a string as a result.

This function could, in principle, be sent many different string arguments at different points in my program so it has no way of knowing, in advance, how long the string will be.

Of course, when I say it receives and returns a string, what I mean is that it receives and returns a pointer to a `char`. So that's how I declare the function return type and the string argument:

ReturnStrings

```
#include <stdio.h>
#include <string.h>
#include <malloc.h>

#define MAXSTRLEN 100

char *string_function(char *astring) {
    char *s;
    s = (char*)malloc(MAXSTRLEN);
    s[0] = '\0';   // I need this to initialize the buffer created by malloc
    strcat(s, "Hello ");
    strcat(s, astring);
    strcat(s, "\n");
    return s;
}

int main(int argc, char **argv) {
    printf(string_function("Fred"));
    printf(string_function("Gussie Fink-Nottle"));
    return 0;
}
```

strcat() or strcat_s()?

`strcat()` is considered to be an 'unsafe' function. Some compilers support more secure alternative functions. The Microsoft compiler, for example, warns that you should use `strcat_s()` instead of `strcat()`. If your compiler recommends a more secure string concatenation function, by all means use it.

Not all compilers support these alternative, more secure functions, however. So, for the sake of compatibility, my code samples will often use 'traditional', widely-supported but sometimes outdated functions such as `strcat()`. In Visual Studio you may either `#define _CRT_SECURE_NO_WARNINGS` in the source code or add it to a property sheet in order to silence the error messages. Other IDEs and compilers may provide other options.

In the *ReturnStrings* project I have defined `MAXSTRLEN` to be 100. I've declared a variable, `s`, within the `string_function()` function to be a pointer to a `char`. As we know, a pointer to a `char` may also be a pointer to an array of `char` – or, to put in another way, it may point to a chunk of memory that stores the series characters in a string:

```
char *s;
```

But before I can store any characters into memory, I need to allocate that memory. I do that using the `malloc()` function. Here I allocate 100 bytes (`MAXSTRLEN` is defined as 100). That's enough for 100 normal alphanumeric characters:

```
s = (char*)malloc(MAXSTRLEN);
```

I initialize a string with the null character by assigning `'\0'` to the first index, 0, of `s`. I need to do that because I want `s` to be a valid (but 'empty') string so that I can concatenate other strings onto it:

```
s[0] = '\0';
```

Then I use the `strcat()` function to concatenate `"Hello "`, the string argument `astring` and a newline `"\n"`:

```
strcat(s, "Hello ");
strcat(s, astring);
strcat(s, "\n");
```

The function returns the string `s` (a pointer to `char`):

```
return s;
```

The Heap and the Stack

It's worth mentioning that `malloc()` allocates memory on the heap. That's important. The local variables declared inside a function are allocated memory in an area called the stack. When you exit from a function, the variables on the stack are cleaned up. To all intents and purposes, they no longer exist when the function exits.

But the heap is where global data is stored in memory. Data assigned to variables on the heap continues to exist even after the program exits from the function in which they were allocated.

That explains why I am able to return a pointer to the string which I created inside the `string_function()` function. Within that function, my code allocated 100 bytes on the heap and stored some characters in that allocated memory.

The characters remain in that allocated memory after the function exits. The function returns a pointer to the address where those characters are stored. That is why, in `main()`, I can access a string (a `char` pointer) that was returned from `string_function()`.

```
int main(int argc, char **argv) {
    printf(string_function("Fred"));
    printf(string_function("Gussie Fink-Nottle"));
    return 0;
}
```

The code in `string_function()` returns a string that begins with `"Hello "`, then the argument that was passed to the function, then a newline. So when the program is run, the code shown above displays:

```
Hello Fred
Hello Gussie Fink-Nottle
```

Everything works correctly as long as I don't try to create a string that has more than 100 characters. But there's a problem. By allocating more memory than I need, I am wasting memory. Every time I call `string_function()`, I allocate 100 bytes. But each string requires a small fraction of that memory.

In a very big program, one that handles large amounts of data, or conversely if I am writing a program for some sort of hardware device that has very small amounts of available memory, wasting memory in this way could be a problem. I'll explain how to avoid that problem later on.

malloc and sizeof

Let's see how to allocate just the right amount of memory to hold an array containing a specific amount of data.

Once again, my program declares a string, s. My aim is to copy a precise number of characters (here, the string "hello") into the memory pointed to by s:

Malloc

```
int main() {
    char *s;
    int stringsize;

    stringsize = sizeof("hello");
    printf("size of 'hello' is %d\n", stringsize);
    s = (char*)malloc(stringsize);
    if (s != NULL) {
        strncpy(s, "hello", stringsize);
        printf("s is %s\n", s);
        s[0] = 'c';
        printf("s is now %s\n", s);
    } else {
        printf("malloc failed!\n");
    }
    return 0;
}
```

I use the `strncpy()` function to copy the characters. As with `strcat()`, your compiler may have alternative and 'safer' functions for copying strings, and you may prefer to use those functions in your own programs. That is not important in this example so I am using the old `strncpy()` function for the sake of compatibility.

The array *into* which I want to copy characters is the first argument, s; the source array – in other words the string I want to copy – is the second argument, "hello". The third argument, `stringsize`, is the number of characters to be copied, which I want to be the size of the string. The question is, how to I calculate the size of the string? That's where `sizeof` comes in.:

```
int stringsize;
stringsize = sizeof("hello");
```

At first sight `sizeof` looks like a regular C function. In fact, it is an operator. It calculates the size of the data – which may be a variable, an array or a structure – placed between parentheses. The value returned is an integer that represents the number of bytes required to store the data.

In this program, I have used `sizeof` to find the number of bytes in the string `"hello"`. I have then called `malloc()` to allocate that exact number of bytes to the `char` pointer `s`.

Cast with malloc()?

In the *Malloc* sample program, I cast the result of `malloc()` to a pointer the type of the data allocated:

```
s = (char*)malloc(stringsize);
```

Strictly speaking this cast isn't necessary because `malloc()` returns a generic pointer. However, I have used it with memory allocation functions such as `malloc()` and `calloc()` to make clear, in the examples, what the allocated memory is used for. In early versions of C, the cast *was* required because `malloc()` returned a `(char *)`. Experienced programmers often omit the cast, and it is entirely a personal preference as to whether you use it or not.

If `malloc()` fails, it will return `NULL`, so I need to check that it has succeeded:

```
if (s != NULL) {
    ...
} else {
    printf("malloc failed!\n");
}
```

Then all being well, I call `strncpy()` to copy the number of characters indicated by `stringsize` from the string `"hello"` into the memory location referenced by the pointer `s`. Whenever you use `malloc()`, you should check the return value for `NULL` but, for brevity, in this book I often omit this check

And finally, just to prove that `s` has been initialized with the characters and is now a valid array of `char`, I've used the normal array-indexing syntax to change the first character, `s[0]`, from `'h'` to `'c'`:

```
printf("s is %s\n", s);
s[0] = 'c';
printf("s is now %s\n", s);
```

And this is what is displayed:

```
s is hello
s is now cello
```

There's one final point I need to mention. I've added this line of code to show the value of `stringsize`, which is the number returned by `sizeof("hello")`:

```
printf("size of 'hello' is %d\n", stringsize);
```

This shows:

```
size of 'hello' is 6
```

At first sight you may think this is wrong because the string `"hello"` has only five characters. In fact, 6 is correct because `sizeof` includes the string terminator, `'\0'`, in its count.

Is sizeof needed?

As a simple `char` is just 1 byte in size these two lines of code are equivalent:

```
s = (char*)malloc(6);
s = (char*)malloc(6 * sizeof(char));
```

But other data types such as doubles, have other sizes so as a rule it is safer to use the `sizeof` operator rather than just guess the number of bytes needed to store some type of data.

calloc

In addition to `malloc()` there is another function, `calloc()`, that is often used when allocating memory. It works just like `malloc()`, but it also performs one additional step – it *clears* the memory. In other words, it initializes the memory with zeros.

Uninitialized memory contains unknown data – junk – which you could accidentally try to use in your program. If you allocate memory with `calloc()`, a series of null characters will be written into that memory (until, of course, you specifically write some other data there).

That allows you to test the allocated memory, if required, so that you know whether or not any specific data – the data you intend it for – has yet been written into that memory.

The only other difference to bear in mind is the syntax: `malloc()` takes a single argument which is the size, in bytes, of the memory required to hold all the data you want to store:

```
s = (char*)malloc(6);
```

`calloc()` takes two arguments: the number of elements in the array and the size, in bytes, of each element. You can calculate the size using the `sizeof` operator:

```
s = (char*)calloc(6, sizeof(char));
```

Consider this example:

Calloc

```
#include <stdio.h>
#include <stdlib.h>
#include <string.h>

int main() {
    char *s;
    int i;
    int *p;

    s = (char*)malloc(6);
    for (i = 0; i < 6; i++) printf("s[%d]=%d\n", i, s[i]);
    free(s);
    s = (char*)calloc(6, sizeof(char));
    for (i = 0; i < 6; i++) printf("s[%d]=%d\n", i, s[i]);
    free(s);
    p = (int*)calloc(6, sizeof(int));
    for (i = 0; i < 6; i++) printf("p[%d]=%d\n", i, p[i]);
    free(p);

    return 0;
}
```

First some memory is allocated with `malloc()`.:

```
s = (char*)malloc(6);
```

The memory allocated by `malloc()` is uninitialized. This `for` loop iterates through it:

```
for (i = 0; i < 6; i++) printf("s[%d]=%d\n", i, s[i]);
```

And it prints out whatever random data happens to be in that block of memory.

```
s[0]=13
s[1]=-16
s[2]=-83
s[3]=-70
s[4]=-64
s[5]=0
```

When I so the same thing with `calloc()`, the memory – that is, the character array to which my `char` pointer points – has been initialized with zeros:

```
s = (char*)calloc(6, sizeof(char));
```

I run this `for` loop:

```
for (i = 0; i < 6; i++) printf("s[%d]=%d\n", i, s[i]);
```

And this time, the null character values (`0`) are printed:

```
s[0]=0
s[1]=0
s[2]=0
s[3]=0
s[4]=0
s[5]=0
```

Similarly, the memory pointed to by my `int` pointer `p`, is initialized with zeros:

```
p = (int*)calloc(6, sizeof(int));
```

I once again run a `for` loop to display the data:

```
for (i = 0; i < 6; i++) printf("p[%d]=%d\n", i, p[i]);
```

And again, the results are predictable – zero values:

```
p[0]=0
p[1]=0
p[2]=0
p[3]=0
p[4]=0
p[5]=0
```

NULL Pointers

Both `malloc()` and `calloc()` return a generic pointer, a pointer to `void`. If the allocation of memory fails they return a `NULL` pointer. It's worth saying what a `NULL` pointer actually is.

A `NULL` pointer is a pointer whose value is `0` – or is may be defined as generic pointer whose value is zero, that is `(void*)0`. In other words, whereas other pointers store a number greater than zero, which is treated as an actual address in memory, by convention a pointer with the value `0` is considered to be one that does not point to a valid address.

We can test for `NULL` pointers in our code. As you may recall I did in the *Malloc* program, earlier in this chapter:

```
if (s == NULL) {
    printf("malloc failed!\n");
    exit(1);
}
```

Memory Leaks

If you glance back at the code of my *Malloc* sample program, you'll see that I used `malloc()` to set aside some memory for a string and I left the memory allocated throughout the program.

Once memory is allocated, it is no longer available to the rest of the program. In principle, if you continue to allocate chunks of memory you might eventually completely run out of memory.

On modern desktop computers, this is rarely the case because modern computers have huge amounts of memory. I could go on allocating more and more memory for strings and rarely run into any problems.

Even so, if you allocated very large amounts of memory without ever freeing any up when it is no longer needed, you would be using memory very inefficiently. Keeping memory allocated when it is no longer needed, (that is, when it is no longer referenced by any variables or pointers in your program), creates what are usually referred to as 'memory leaks'.

This could be a real problem if you happen to be writing C programs for devices that don't have huge amounts of memory. For example, hardware microcontrollers or robotic devices might have very small amounts of memory.

At any rate, it is good practice to deallocate and 'reclaim' memory that isn't in use. That makes the memory available to store other data as needed. The usual way to do that in C is by calling the `free()` function.

Freeing Memory

Look at this code from the *Calloc* sample program:

Calloc

```
s = (char*)malloc(6);
for (i = 0; i < 6; i++) printf("s[%d]=%d\n", i, s[i]);
free(s);
```

Here I allocate memory for an array of six characters. Then, when I no longer need that array, I call `free()`, passing to it the variable for which the memory was allocated. Here that is the string `s`.

Here is another example with the `int` pointer `p`:

```
p = (int*)calloc(6, sizeof(int));
for (i = 0; i < 6; i++) printf("p[%d]=%d\n", i, p[i]);
free(p);
```

You should make a habit of freeing memory when it is no longer needed. But be careful. If you call `free()` on a variable that was never allocated, or if you try to use allocated memory after you have called `free()`, your program will go horribly wrong. We'll look at these types of problems in the final chapter of this book.

realloc

Sometimes you may want to change the size of a block of allocated memory. To do that you can use `realloc()`. Here, for example, I have allocated enough memory to hold the string `"hello"`. That's six bytes, as calculated by `sizeof`: the 5 visible characters plus the null character terminator:

```
char *s;
int i;

i = sizeof("hello");
s = (char*)malloc(i);
strncpy(s, "hello", i);
printf("s is %s\n", s);
```

But now I decide I want to display the longer string `"hello world"`. What do I do? Just concatenate `"world"` onto the end of the existing string likes this?

```
strcat(s, " world");
```

No! If I do that I am heading towards disaster.

My program will, at best, malfunction (it will display 'junk' characters) and, at worst, it may even crash.

This is the error message that Microsoft C shows when I try to debug this program:

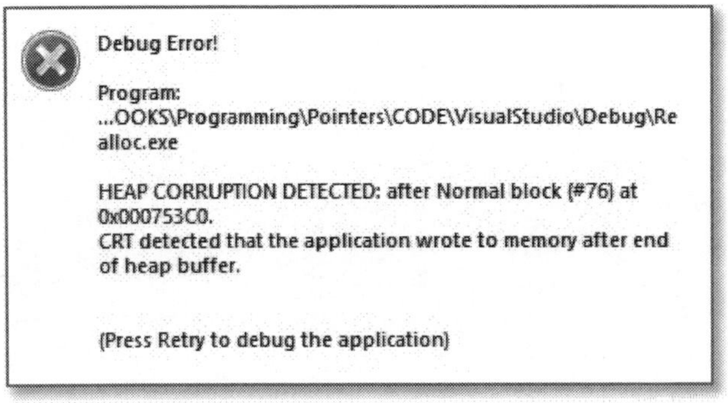

That's because I have only allocated enough memory for the string `"hello"`. But I've tried to copy a larger string into that memory. And, quite simply, insufficient memory has been set aside to hold this larger string. That won't work. I have to allocate memory first.

Let's see how to do that. The string `"hello world"` contains twelve characters: 5 in `"hello"`, 1 for the space, 5 for `"world"` and 1 for the null string terminator. So I need to allocate twelve bytes of memory.

I can do that by calling `realloc()` with the pointer to the previously allocated block of memory, which here is the `char` pointer `s`, as the first argument; and the new size in bytes, here `12`, as the second argument:

```
s = (char*)realloc(s, 12);
```

Now it is safe to store the longer string. All I need to do is concatenate the new string (`"world"`) since `realloc()` will copy any existing data (`"hello"`) into the new memory area:

```
strcat(s, " world");
```

5 – Pointer Arithmetic

In some of the short programs we've looked at in this book, I've iterated over the items in an array just by adding 1 to the pointer variable. What happens when I do that?

What is Pointer Arithmetic?

Here's an example, taken from the *MultipleIndirection* program in Chapter 3. I add 1 to `pi`, a pointer to an integer, in order to move to the next element in an array of integers:

```
pi += 1;
```

But wait a minute, since the value of a pointer is a number that represents an address in memory, why does adding 1 to a pointer have the effect of moving it to the next element in an array?

Maybe it's because it just increases the value by one byte so it moves the pointer one byte in memory and that's where the next element in the array is stored?

But no, that doesn't make sense either. I know that my C compiler needs 4 bytes for an integer. So it would seem that when I add 1 to my `int` pointer I actually cause it to move 4 bytes in memory to point to the next `int` in my array. This is an example of 'pointer arithmetic' which is also sometimes called 'address arithmetic'.

How big is an int?

In principle, an `int` could be stored in 2 bytes. In practice, most 32-bit or 64-bit C compilers store an `int` in 4-bytes. Other integer types may require varying numbers of bytes. For example a `short` typically requires 2 bytes and a `long` requires 4 bytes. If in doubt use the `sizeof` operator to return the size of a data-type.

To understand what is really going on here we need to look at how pointer arithmetic is done in C. Here, is my *AddressArithmetic1* sample program. In the version supplied in the code archive this program also includes numerous `printf()` statements and comments, which I've omitted from this listing for clarity:

AddressArithmetic1

```
#include <stdio.h>
#include <stdlib.h>
#include <string.h>

#define COUNT 4

int main() {
    int *p;
    int a[COUNT];

    for (int i = 0; i < COUNT; i++) a[i] = i;

    p = a;
    p = p + 1;
    p = p + 2;
    p = p + 1;

    return 0;
}
```

In this program, I create an array of 4 integers. Since I have declared the array's size at the time of its declaration (shown below), memory will automatically be allocated for it on the stack so I don't need to call the `malloc()` function:

```
int a[COUNT];
```

In the `for` loop I initialize the array with four integers from `0` to `3`:

```
for (int i = 0; i < COUNT; i++) a[i] = i;
```

I set the `p` pointer to point to it – that is, by assigning the array `a` to the pointer `p`, I set the *value* of `p` to the *address* of `a`:

```
p = a;
```

This is now the situation. Pointer `p` points to the address of the array, `a`. The address of `a` is also the address where the first integer, `0`, is located. The diagram that follows shows this…

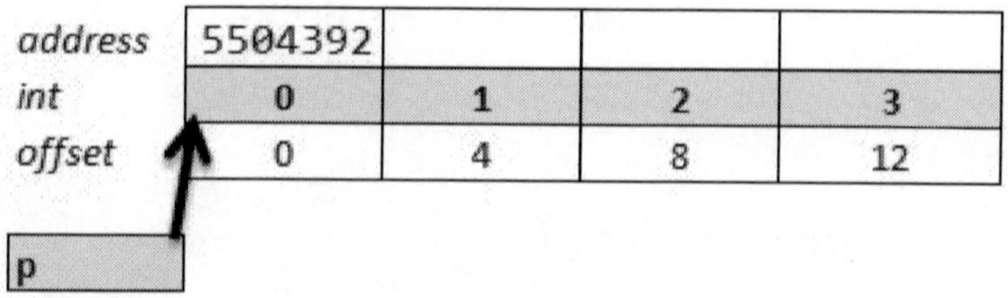

In the code of this project from the code archive, I have this `printf()` statement:

```
printf("address of a is %p; value of p is %p [%d]; value pointed to by p is d\n",
    a, p, p, *p);
```

This is what is displayed:

```
address of a is 0053FD88; value of p is 0053FD88 [5504392]; value pointed to by p
is 0
```

This first shows the address of the array `a`, and the value of the pointer `p`. They are the same (`0053FD88` in hexadecimal or `5504392` in decimal), as you would expect.

Then I dereference `p` (that is, I print `*p` as a decimal value) which shows me the integer to which `p` points. It is `0`, the first element of the array. Then I add 1 to the pointer variable `p`:

```
p = p + 1;
```

Once again, I print some information:

```
address of a is 0053FD88; value of p is 0053FD8C [5504396]; value pointed to by p
is 1
```

The pointer `p` now points to the second element, `1`, in the array:

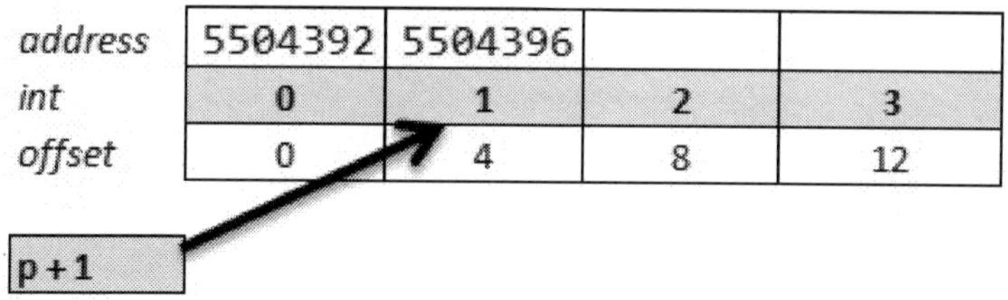

The address of the array never changes so this is the same number as before (0053FD88). The value of the pointer p has changed, however. Before I added 1 to it, the value was 0053FD88 in hexadecimal, which is the same as 5504392 in decimal. But now its value is 0053FD8C which is 5504396 in decimal.

Decimal pointer values?

As I mentioned earlier, by tradition, pointer values in C are shown in hexadecimal. I've also used decimal format here (even though it's possible that your compiler may object) because, unless you are very familiar with hexadecimal numbers, decimals make it much easier to understand exactly what is going on.

Adding 1 to p has increased its value by 4. That's 4 bytes. Which is the size on an integer! As p is pointing to an array of integers it now pointing to a location 4-bytes from the start of the array. When I dereference p I see that it points to the second element of the array, the integer 1.

Incrementing Pointers

Why does adding 1 to the pointer p increase its value by 4? It's because C knows that the array a to which p points contains integers. That's how I declared it.

```
int *p;
int a[COUNT];

for (int i = 0; i < COUNT; i++) a[i] = i;
p = a;
```

It knows that an int takes up 4 bytes and so it also knows that when I add 1 to my pointer, what I mean to do is to increase the value of that pointer (that is, to increment the address that it stores) by however many bytes are required in order to move to the next element of the array. In this case, since the array stores integers, it must move one integer's size through memory to get to the next integer in the array.

Now I add another 2 to the pointer:

```
p = p + 2;
```

Remember, I previously added 1 to p. So when I add another 2, the original value of p has been increased by 3. That's 3 * 4 since 4 is the size of an int.

I print out the same range of information as before:

```
address of a is 0053FD88; value of p is 0053FD94 [5504404]; value pointed to by p
is 3
```

I can see that the value of `p` – the address to which it points – has been increased (as expected) by 8; that is, twice the size of an `int`.

It was previously pointing to the first element in the array. Now it points to the fourth element (two more `int`'s worth of memory), which is the integer `3`.

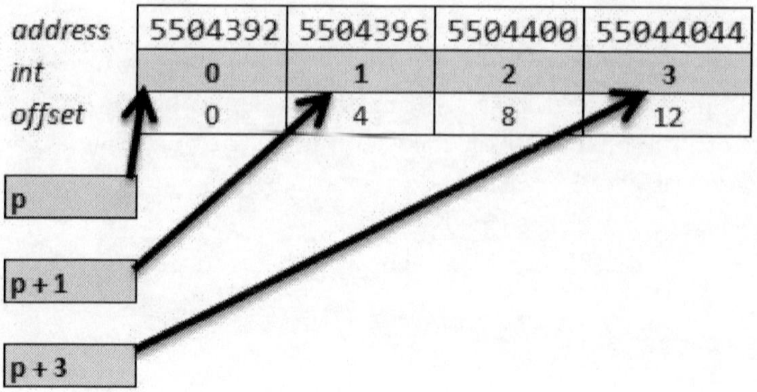

Finally, I decide to see what will happen if I increment the pointer once again:

```
p = p + 1;
```

It was already pointing to the final element in the array, so what will it point to now?

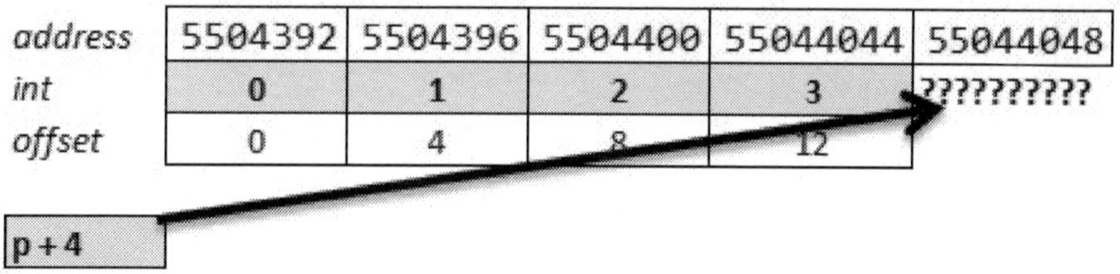

The answer that that question is – well, your guess is as good as mine. This is what I see when I print the value stored at the address to which `p` now points:

```
address of a is 0053FD88; value of p is 0053FD98 [5504408]; value pointed to by p
is -858993460
```

The pointer p now points to whatever happens to be in the memory four bytes *after the end of the array*. The value here (-858993460) makes no real sense. The fact of the matter is that I shouldn't really be trying to access that memory at all because it has not been allocated for my array.

In a real-world program, you would need to check that any pointer arithmetic operations only access known memory locations – such as an index in an array which you have previously allocated and initialized.

Calculating an Array Index

Pointer arithmetic doesn't work solely with arrays of integers. As long as C knows what the data type of an array is, it is able to calculate the appropriate number of bytes needed to move from one element to the next. Look at the example on the next page.

In the *AddressArithmetic2* project I've declared these arrays:

AddressArithmetic2

```
#define COUNT 4

int a[COUNT];
float b[COUNT];
double c[COUNT];
long long int d[COUNT];
short int e[COUNT];
long int f[COUNT];
```

In the main() function I have declared pointers to a variety of different data types:

```
int *pa;
float *pb;
double *pc;
long long int *pd;
short int *pe;
long int *pf;
```

I then assign the address of each array to a pointer of the corresponding data type:

```
pa = a;
pb = b;
pc = c;
pd = d;
pe = e;
pf = f;
```

This is the complete *AddressArithmetic2* project. However, this listing omits some comments and `printf()` statements which you will find in the version supplied in the source code archive:

AddressArithmetic2

```
#define COUNT 4

int a[COUNT];
float b[COUNT];
double c[COUNT];
long long int d[COUNT];
short int e[COUNT];
long int f[COUNT];

int main() {
    int *pa;
    float *pb;
    double *pc;
    long long int *pd;
    short int *pe;
    long int *pf;

    pa = a;
    pb = b;
    pc = c;
    pd = d;
    pe = e;
    pf = f;
    for (int i = 0; i < COUNT; i++) {
        a[i] = i;
        b[i] = (float)i;
        c[i] = (double)i;
        d[i] = i;
        e[i] = i;
        f[i] = i;
    }
    pa += 1;
    pb += 1;
    pc += 1;
    pd += 1;
    pe += 1;
    pf += 1;
    return 0;
}
```

I fill the arrays with some data:

```
for (int i = 0; i < COUNT; i++) {
    a[i] = i;
    b[i] = (float)i;
    c[i] = (double)i;
    d[i] = i;
    e[i] = i;
    f[i] = i;
}
```

Finally, I do some simple pointer arithmetic by adding 1 to each pointer variable:

```
pa += 1;
pb += 1;
pc += 1;
pd += 1;
pe += 1;
pf += 1;
return 0;
```

Right at the end of the code I have some `printf()` statements (these are not shown in the listing on the previous page but you will find them in the code in the archive) to display some information on the addresses and values of the arrays and pointers.

Once again, I've shown addresses in the 'conventional' hexadecimal format (using `"%p"` in the format string shown by `printf()`), and also its decimal representation (using `"%d"`). The decimal versions of the addresses make it easier to count the number of bytes between one address and another. The decimal addresses are shown between square brackets.

```
address of a is 002BA630 [2860592]; value of pa is 002BA634 [2860596]; value
pointed to by pa is 1

address of b is 002BA620 [2860576]; value of pb is 002BA624 [2860580]; value
pointed to by pb is 1.000000

address of c is 002BA600 [2860544]; value of pc is 002BA608 [2860552]; value
pointed to by pc is 1.000000

address of d is 002BA5E0 [2860512]; value of pd is 002BA5E8 [2860520]; value
pointed to by pd is 1

address of e is 002BA5D0 [2860496]; value of pe is 002BA5D2 [2860498]; value
pointed to by pe is 1

address of f is 002BA5C0 [2860480]; value of pf is 002BA5C4 [2860484]; value
pointed to by pf is 1
```

Now, you can see that adding 1 to the pointer variables has the effect of moving the pointer to point to the element at the next index of each array.

Look at the array address. Then look at the address of the next element – that is, the result of adding 1 to the pointer variable. In each case the difference is the same as the size of the data type. Using the Microsoft C compiler on Windows, these are the sizes of each data type.

4	`int`
4	`float`
8	`double`
8	`long long int`
2	`short int`
4	`long int`

On some platforms, and with some C compilers, the sizes of data types may be different from the ones shown here. For instance, when I ran the *AddressArithmetic2* program on a Mac I noticed that a `long int` had a size of 8 bytes, not 4 as on Windows.

However, when I use pointer arithmetic, I don't have to worry about the actual sizes of any given data type because I don't have to calculate the 'offset' (the number of bytes from the start of an array to a given element) myself. When I add a value to a pointer variable, the offset is calculated for me.

That means I can write some C code on Windows then compile and run it on my Mac without making any changes at all. Because the Mac compiler calculates an 8 byte offset for my array of `long int` numbers. So when I do my pointer arithmetic, by adding 1 to the pointer variable, it moves 8 bytes in memory (rather than the 4 bytes required on my Windows PC), to reference the next element of the array.

6 – Pointers to Structs

In some earlier programs I showed how you can allocate a specific amount of memory to hold data of a specific size. For example, this is how I uses the `realloc()` function to allocate twelves bytes for the string, s:

Realloc

```
s = (char*)realloc(s, 12);
```

Allocating a fixed number of bytes like this is all well and good in a simple demonstration program. But in a real world program, it's a very bad idea. That's because the size of some data types may vary according to which compiler or operating system you are using.

Varying data sizes

It is not safe to assume a size even for 'simple' types. Remember, in the last chapter we saw that a `long int` is 4 bytes on Windows and 8 bytes on a Mac. With more complex data types, such as structs, you should never assume you know how much memory is actually required.

What is the Size of a struct?

Let's look at a program using structs. Let's suppose I define the `struct` named `MYSTRUCT` shown below. I've noted the sizes of the data types of each field in comments:

```
typedef struct {
    int a;          // 4 bytes
    int c;          // 4 bytes
    double b;       // 8 bytes
    long long int d; // 8 bytes
} MYSTRUCT;
```

To work out how much memory is needed to store a `MYSTRUCT struct` I just add up the sizes of the data-types it contains: 4+4+8+8. The result is 24 bytes. Just in case there is any doubt, I can verify the size:

```
printf("size of MYSTRUCT = %d\n", sizeof(MYSTRUCT));
```

Yes, it's 24 bytes:

```
size of MYSTRUCT = 24
```

So now I can just create a pointer to a `MYSTRUCT struct` and allocate 24 bytes like this, can't I?

```
MYSTRUCT *p;
p = (MYSTRUCT*)calloc(COUNT, 24);
```

Wrong!

But *why* is this wrong? After all, we've just seen that my program runs fine.

Well then, if it isn't wrong, for the time being, it is at any rate a very, *very* bad idea. Let me show you why. Let's say I decide to reorder the fields of my `struct`. After all, `c` should logically come after `b`, shouldn't it? So let me do that.

You'll find this code in the *AddressArithmetic3* project:

AddressArithmetic3

```
typedef struct {
    int a;              // 4 bytes
    double b;           // 8 bytes
    int c;              // 4 bytes
    long long int d; // 8 bytes
} MYSTRUCT;
```

This is a trivial change. It's just a matter of tidying up the code slightly. So I don't bother testing it again. It's the end of a long, hard day and I'm very happy with the work I've done. I send my program back out into the world. And when I get back to my desk the next morning, everyone's going nuts. Because my program keeps crashing.

Why?

Let's run the program again.

When I run this code with Microsoft C in Visual Studio, this is what I see:

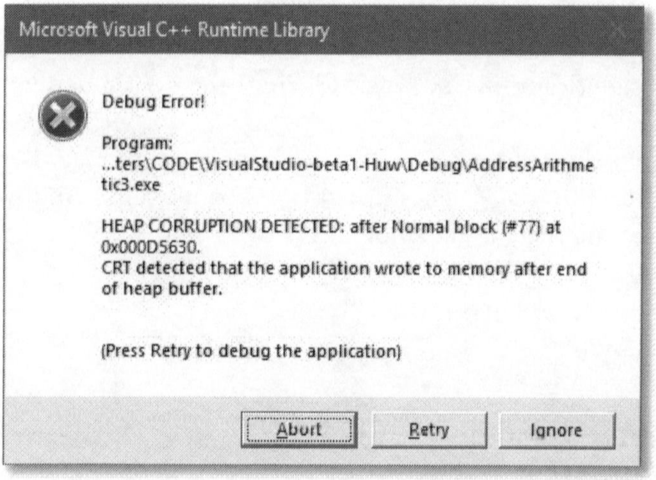

What? No Error?

The actual error message you see may be different than the one Visual Studio showed me. It is even possible that you may see no error message at all. In fact, when I ran or debugged this code at different times using both the Microsoft and GCC (Gnu Compiler Collection) compilers and debuggers I saw several error messages, caused by errors at different points in the program. The Microsoft C runtime generates the error when I try to free the pointer – `free(p)` – but GCC bombs out earlier in the code. Even if you run the code with no error message shown, that doesn't alter the fact that your program has malfunctioned and even if a crash doesn't happen right away, it may happen later on!

At the moment we are running a very short, very simple bit of code. But in principle this error might have occurred somewhere deep inside a big, complex, mission-critical program: an international banking system, say, or an airline ticket-booking system. So having it crash unexpectedly is absolutely not acceptable.

Field Order in a struct

Why did the program crash?

I didn't change anything significant, did I? I just tidied up the `struct` definition by re-ordering the fields.

It turns out that reordering the fields of a `struct` *is* a significant change. Because, strange as it may seem, my `struct` no longer takes up 24 bytes of memory. And when I allocate 24 bytes, I am not allocating the correct amount. Look, I run this code again:

```
printf("size of MYSTRUCT = %d\n", sizeof(MYSTRUCT));
```

This is what I see:

```
size of MYSTRUCT = 32
```

sizeof to the Rescue

This is why you should always use `sizeof` to calculate the actual size of a piece of data rather than assuming you know its size.

Let me delete this line of code:

```
p = (MYSTRUCT*)calloc(COUNT,  24);
```

And I replace it with this:

```
p = (MYSTRUCT*)calloc(COUNT, sizeof(MYSTRUCT));
```

And now when I run or debug the program my code works. I get no error message. And, what's even better, this time I can be confident that I have allocated the right amount of memory even if I, or someone else, decides to reorder the fields of my `struct`, or even add new fields to it. Because no matter what the size of the `struct` may be, `sizeof` returns the correct value when memory needs to be allocated.

Why Did the struct Size Change?

So we've established that the size of my `struct` changes when I change the order of its fields. When the fields are in *this* order, the `struct` takes up 24 bytes:

```
typedef struct {
    int a;              // 4 bytes
    int c;              // 4 bytes
    double b;           // 8 bytes
    long long int d;    // 8 bytes
} MYSTRUCT;
```

But when the fields are in *this* order, the `struct` takes up 32 bytes:

```
typedef struct {
    int a;              // 4 bytes
    double b;           // 8 bytes
    int c;              // 4 bytes
    long long int d;    // 8 bytes
} MYSTRUCT;
```

And yet, in each case the `struct` contains the same data (two lots of 4 bytes, two lots of 8 bytes) which, when I add up the sizes comes to a total of 24. So where have the extra bytes come from? To understand that you have to understand how the C compiler *aligns* the data in memory.

Data Type Alignment

The size of my `struct` was different when I changed the order of its fields because its size depends on the way the data fields are aligned in memory.

Alignment is not obvious

When discussing data type alignment, I am assuming you are using an Intel-based desktop computer. The way data types are arranged in memory may be different on other architectures such an ARM processor or a microcontroller. As a general rule, it is best to make no assumptions about how data is stored and always check the actual size of a data type before allocating memory.

What is Data Alignment?

To understand data alignment, imagine that I am storing my `struct` in a matrix of cells, like in a spreadsheet.

A	A	A	A				
B	B	B	B	B	B	B	B
C	C	C	C				
D	D	D	D	D	D	D	D

- The `int A` takes 4 bytes.
- The `double B` takes 8 bytes.
- The `int C` takes 4 bytes.
- The `long long int D` takes 8 bytes.

These data fields are arranged in memory much as I've arranged them in the cells of my spreadsheet. They form a nice, neat, regular matrix. It's not exactly the way memory is arranged in your computer but it might be useful to imagine it that way.

The fields of the `struct` are aligned so that they all start at predefined boundaries. An 8 byte data type such as B (`double`) or D (`long long int`) is aligned so it starts at an 8-byte boundary.

To visualise that in a spreadsheet, if I start counting along the cells in my matrix of cells, each 8-byte data type needs to start at some multiple of 8-bytes of memory from the start of the matrix. I count the cells – the bytes – used by A: 1,2,3,4. Then I get to cell 5 in the first row. But my double, B, can't start here, where the 4-byte `int` ends because that's a 4-byte boundary.

So I carry on counting along the 4 empty cells in the first row (or unused bytes in memory): 5,6,7,8. These empty cells to the right of A aren't used but they *are* important. They are there to *pad out the gap* between the 4-byte `int` (A) and the 8-byte `double` (B) to ensure that the `double` starts at an 8-byte boundary.

In my code I have used the `calloc()` function to allocate memory:

```
p = (MYSTRUCT*)calloc(COUNT, sizeof(MYSTRUCT));
```

As I explained in Chapter 4, `calloc()` initializes memory with zeros. So the memory locations that aren't initialized with data from the fields of my `struct` will contain zeros. It isn't an absolute requirement to initialize memory in this way but it's a good idea to do so and makes debugging easier because at least their values are predictable. I can represent this in my spreadsheet by showing null characters in the 'empty' cells:

A	A	A	A	\0	\0	\0	\0
B	B	B	B	B	B	B	B
C	C	C	C	\0	\0	\0	\0
D	D	D	D	D	D	D	D

Think of this `struct` as occupying a matrix of 4 'rows' by 8 'columns'. The matrix needs to be 8 columns (or bytes) wide in order to accommodate the largest of the data types in the `struct`: the `double` (B) and `long long int` (D) plus some padding (the unused bytes) after the two smaller `int` fields (A and C). Hence, my `struct` takes up 4 multiplied by 8. That's 32 bytes.

But when I rearrange the field order, by putting the two `int` fields one after the other, the C compiler can optimize its use of memory. Instead of padding out the first `int`, A, with extra bytes, it just puts the *next* data field, which is now another `int`, C, alongside it. The two 4-byte fields fit neatly into this matrix and no unused 'padding' is needed to align the 8-byte data fields at 8-byte boundaries:

A	A	A	A	C	C	C	C
B	B	B	B	B	B	B	B
D	D	D	D	D	D	D	D

So the matrix now takes 8 fewer cells in my spreadsheet – or 8 fewer bytes in memory. My spreadsheet now has 3 rows and 8 columns. Multiply 3 by 8. That's 24. So my `struct` now takes up 24 bytes in memory.

Type Alignment on Boundaries

In summary, this is how data alignment works. Data types of a certain size are aligned on boundaries of that size. A 4 byte `int` is aligned on a 4-byte boundary whereas an 8-byte `double` is aligned on an 8 byte boundary and so on.

Look again at this `struct`:

```
typedef struct {
    int a;             // 4 bytes
    double b;          // 8 bytes
    int c;             // 4 bytes
    long long int d; // 8 bytes
} MYSTRUCT;
```

If a single 4-byte `int` immediately precedes an 8-byte double, as it does in my `struct`, 4 extra bytes are added after the `int` to ensure that the 8-byte `double` starts on an 8-byte boundary. That is, at a multiple of 8 bytes from the start of the `struct`: with boundaries at 8, 16, 24 bytes and so on. But when two 4-byte `int`s occur one after the other, they end at a natural 8-byte boundary. That's what happens in this version of my `struct`:

```
typedef struct {
    int a;             // 4 bytes
    int c;             // 4 bytes
    double b;          // 8 bytes
    long long int d; // 8 bytes
} MYSTRUCT;
```

In this case, the `double` is already aligned on a 8-byte boundary, so no extra padding is needed.

Natural alignment

When some data is said to be 'aligned' on an X-byte boundary, each piece of data is stored at an address that is an integer multiple of X. This is sometimes called 'natural alignment'. On most computers, the reading and writing of data is most efficient when data is 'naturally aligned' – that is, when the address of each data element is a multiple of the size of that piece of data.

Never Assume the Size of Data Types

The really important lesson you need to learn from this is that *the size of data types cannot be assumed.* With different compilers on different architectures, even simple data types might take up different amounts of memory. So if you allocate a specific number of bytes when you write your code on one computer the program may not work correctly when it is deployed on another computer or some other device or microcontroller.

If you use complex data types, such as structs, the situation becomes even more error prone. The way structs are stored in memory is not predictable across different machine architectures. As I've shown here, even making an apparently trivial change to a struct, by reordering its fields, may change the amount of memory it needs.

Alignment of memory

To a programmer, memory can appear as a simple array of bytes, starting at zero and ending at some very large number. But to the computer hardware, that's not how it looks at all. There are many factors involved to make this nice simple 'programmer' view work. It turns out that for speed, some data in this apparently simple array need to be aligned at 4, 8 or other powers of two. If you don't align things correctly, your program may well run more slowly or may not work at all.

Structs and Pointer Arithmetic

In the last chapter we did pointer arithmetic with simple numeric data types. In fact, pointer arithmetic also works with more complicated types such a structs. This is how to do it.

Calculate the Size of the Data type

Use the `sizeof` operator to calculate the amount of memory needed for a `struct`: `sizeof(MYSTRUCT)`

Allocate Memory for an Array of struct

Define a pointer to a defined `struct` then allocate the correct amount of memory for a specific number of structs. Here I allocate enough memory for four `MYSTRUCT` structs:

AddressArithmetic3

```
#define COUNT 4
MYSTRUCT *p, *q;
p = (MYSTRUCT*)calloc(COUNT, sizeof(MYSTRUCT));
```

Do the Pointer Arithmetic

When you do pointer arithmetic you can let the compiler work out how many bytes are needed to go to the next element in an array. It doesn't matter whether the array contains integers, doubles, chars or structs, the pointer arithmetic works in exactly the same way.

If you have a pointer to an array of 4-byte integers and you add 1 to the pointer variable, the pointer will now reference the next element in the array – that is, the element 4 bytes along from the previous element.

If you have a pointer to an array of 24-byte structs and you add 1 to the pointer variable, this pointer will also reference the next element in the array – but this time it will be the element 24 bytes along from the previous element.

Here, for example, the pointer `q` adds 3 to the pointer `p` in order to reference the fourth `struct` in the array (recall the first `struct` is at index 0) to which `p` points:

```
q = p;
q = p + 3;
```

Don't Do Pointer Arithmetic with Generic Pointers

This sort of pointer arithmetic only works with arrays of specific data types. You can't do pointer arithmetic with generic pointers – pointers to `void` – unless they are first cast to a known type. Let's assume that I set the generic pointer `v` to point to the fourth element of the `MYSTRUCT` array to which `p` points:

```
void *v;
v = p + 3;
```

I cannot now simply use `v` as a pointer to `MYSTRUCT`. I cannot index into the array like this: `v[3]`. And I can't do pointer arithmetic like this: `v = v + 3`. That's because the compiler doesn't know the actual data type to which `v` points.

So *this* works fine (because the compiler knows the pointer type of `q`):

```
MYSTRUCT *p, *q;
q = p + 3;
printf("v->a %d\n", q->a);
```

But *this* won't work:

```
MYSTRUCT *p;
void* v;
v = p + 3;
printf("v->a %d\n", q->a);      // This is incorrect
```

This, however, *will* work (because I explicitly cast v to point to MYSTRUCT, so the compiler now knows (since I've told it, using the cast) what data type it is working with:

```
printf("v->a %d\n", ((MYSTRUCT*)v)->a);
```

Arrays of Structs May be Padded

Before we leave this subject, let's finally consider the implications of an array of structs in which the structs may not be completely 'filled' with data.

This would occur when some of the contiguous data fields contain data of different sizes as was the case in the version of MYSTRUCT that defined an int (4 bytes), followed by a double (8 bytes), then an int (4 bytes) then a long long int (8 bytes);

A	A	A	A	\0	\0	\0	\0
B	B	B	B	B	B	B	B
C	C	C	C	\0	\0	\0	\0
D	D	D	D	D	D	D	D

The memory between the 4-byte fields and the 8-byte fields that follow is unused. If I allocate memory using the calloc() function, this unused memory will be filled with zeros as shown above.

Let's consider how you might use pointer arithmetic to move through the memory used to store a struct in 4-byte increments. Here I'll use my generic pointer, v. I'll use this inside a for loop:

```
for (int i = 0; i < sizeof(MYSTRUCT) / sizeof(int); i++) {
    printf("v[%d]=%d\n", i, ((int*)v)[i]);
}
```

At each turn through the loop I need to increment v by the size of MYSTRUCT divided by the size of an int. While I am going to use the sizeof operator to calculate these sizes (for reasons already explained), in order to help you understand what is happening here, I am going to assume that the size of `MYSTRUCT` is 32 bytes and the size of `int` is 4.

So this loop will run while `i` is less than 32/4: that is, 8. It will move through the data of a single `MYSTRUCT struct` in eight 4-byte chunks:

```
for (int i = 0; i < sizeof(MYSTRUCT) / sizeof(int); i++)
```

I want to display an integer representation of the 4-bytes at each memory location. Remember, a generic pointer can't be used to do pointer arithmetic or array indexing. So this won't work:

```
printf("v[%d]=%d\n", i, v[i]);          // Won't work!
```

But when I cast `v` as a pointer to `int` I will be able to use ordinary array indexing in order to get at an `int`-sized (4-byte) chunk of data, which is what I do in the `for` loop:

```
printf("v[%d]=%d\n", i, ((int*)v)[i]);
```

Earlier in the program, I set the pointer `v` to point to the fourth element in the array (`v = p + 3`). The `struct` at that position has been initialized this this data:

```
a (int)                = 3
b (double)             = 10000000003.000000
c (int)                = 60
d (long long int)      = 4294967299
```

And this is what the `printf()` in my `for` loop displays:

```
v[0]=3
v[1]=0
v[2]=538443776
v[3]=1107468383
v[4]=60
v[5]=0
v[6]=3
v[7]=1
```

We needn't be concerned by the values shown for indexes 2 and 3, or 6 and 7. In each case the data stored here requires 8 bytes, so displaying it in 4-byte chunks won't mean very much. What is more important is to notice the 'empty' chunk of memory that immediately follows each of the `int` data fields.

Consider the values displayed at these specific indexes:

```
v[0]=3
v[1]=0
v[4]=60
v[5]=0
```

The first `int` (`a`) takes up the first four bytes right at the start of the `struct` (`v[0]`). This has the value 3.

Because the `struct` is aligned on 8-byte boundaries (to accommodate the 8-byte `double` and `long long int` fields), this leaves 4-bytes of unused memory between the `int` (`a`) and the `double` (`b`) that follows it.

Since I allocated memory with `calloc()` the unused memory has been filled with zeros. So when my loop displays the data at `v[1]`, it shows the value `0`.

This zero is the 'padding' between field `a` and field `b` of the `struct`. You can see that the same padding occurs between the `int` field `c` (`v[4]`) and the `long long int` that follows it: that is why we find another `0` at index `v[5]`.

In Summary

If you fail to obey the rules for data alignment, your program may run into problems. It might not run correctly or it may not produce the results that you expect. It may even crash completely. The important lesson to learn is that you should never make assumptions about data alignment. For example, you should not assume that a structure is of a predictable size. Instead, you should explicitly use `sizeof` to obtain the actual size. In that way, you can avoid unexpected problems before they occur.

7 – Lists and Data Structures

Arrays are convenient ways of storing lists of data items. In many cases, a simple array may be all you need whenever you want to create a linear list of items. But arrays have some disadvantages. The most obvious of these is that an array has a fixed length. If I declare an array for five elements I can't add a sixth onto the end of it. Once an array has been created its size cannot be changed.

A workaround would be to create an array much bigger than I think I will ever need. So I might declare an array capable of storing 100 elements but only initialize it with 20. That gives me the option of adding another 80 elements if I happen to need them. But this is obviously inefficient and, in any case, my initial estimate might be wrong. I might need to add 81 new elements, in which case I have a problem.

One solution to this problem is to create a linked list instead of an array.

Arrays and Linked lists

How is a linked list different from an array? Before discussing that, let's first be sure that we understand exactly what array is.

Arrays

Let's suppose I have an array of five integers: 1, 2, 3, 4, 5. I could think of this is being a bit like a row of spreadsheet cells. Each cell represents a chunk of memory sufficient to hold a single element of a certain type. Here that would be four bytes of memory for each integer.

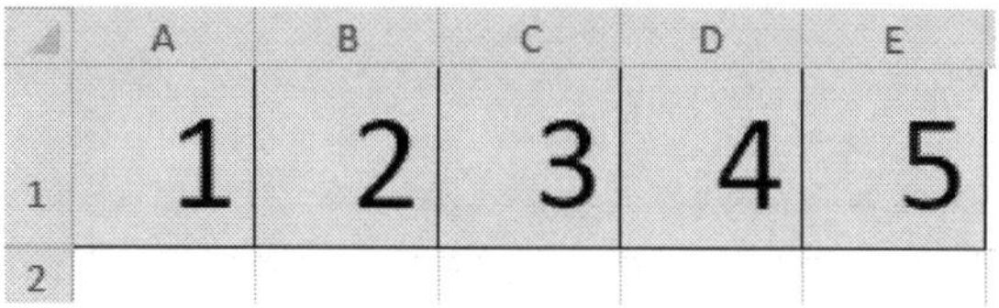

Before I add any elements to my array I have to allocate enough memory to hold a fixed number of data items. Each chunk of memory for each element of the array starts where the previous chunk of memory ends.

Linked Lists

A linked list isn't like that at all. When I create a linked list I don't allocate a fixed block of memory in advance. Instead, I allocate memory on an element-by-element basis.

If I create a list that contains two elements, I allocate just enough memory to hold two elements. If I now want to add a third element onto the list, I allocate another chunk of memory for that new element and then add that element to my list.

As I'm adding, and maybe deleting, elements at various different points during the execution of my program, I can't guarantee that those elements will all be stored in a contiguous block of memory, as they would be in an array. In fact, in all probability their locations in memory (their addresses) will be scattered around all over the place like this:

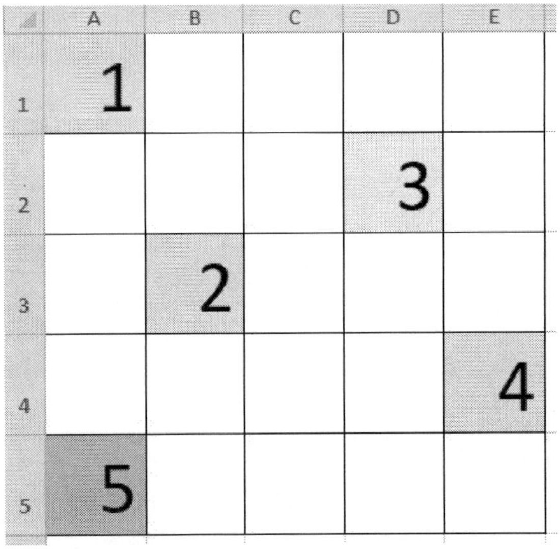

As these items don't occupy a single sequential block of memory, I can't just iterate through memory by counting along a certain number of bytes, as I did when using pointer arithmetic or by using array indexing with square brackets.

Linking Elements in a List

How then does *Element 1* in my list know where *Element 2* can be found?

It does so using a pointer to *Element 2*. The 'links' in a linked list are actually pointers to other list elements. The pointer in *Element 1* stores the address of *Element 2*. So if I know where *Element 1* is, I can use the pointer in *Element 1* to find *Element 2*.

In my spreadsheet, the cell at the address `A1` represents a `struct` (*Element 1*) that contains the integer data `1` and a pointer to the `struct` (*Element 2*) at the address `B3`.

From *Element 2*, I can use a pointer to find *Element 3* and so on. Non-contiguous structs in memory are analogous to non-adjacent cells in a spreadsheet. In a spreadsheet I can access another cell (for example, in a formula) using its location – the address of the cell. That's kind of how a linked list works. In C, a `struct` can contain both some *data* and a *pointer* that gives the address of the next `struct` in the list.

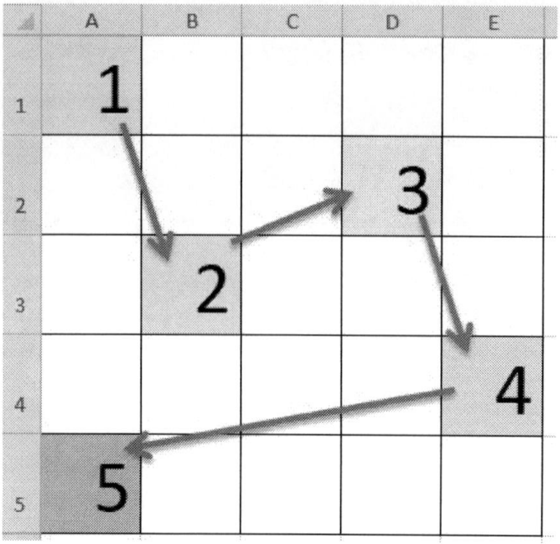

Singly-linked lists

A 'singly-linked' list is a list in which each element contains a single pointer whose value is the address of (or, in other words, a 'link' to) another element in the list. Here's an example of a linked list of integers.

SingleLinkedList

```
#include <stdio.h>
#include <stdlib.h>
#include <string.h>

typedef struct listitem {
    struct listitem *next;     // pointer to next item
    int data;                  // some data
} LISTITEM;

int main() {
    LISTITEM *listhead, *temp;

    listhead = NULL;

    for (int i = 0; i < 3; i++) {
        temp = (LISTITEM*)malloc(sizeof(LISTITEM));
        temp->data = i;
        temp->next = listhead;
        listhead = temp;
    }

    temp = listhead;
    while (temp != NULL) {
        printf("list item: \n\tcurrent is %p\n\tnext is %p\n\tdata is %d\n",
            temp, temp->next, temp->data);
        temp = temp->next;
    }
    return 0;
}
```

As mentioned earlier (Chapter 4) with modern C compilers a type-cast with `malloc()` is optional – though it was a requirement with older C compilers. I use the cast `(LISTITEM*)` here for code clarity. Incidentally, in the C++ language, the cast is required.

The `listitem struct` has a `data` field – which here is a simple `int` – and a `next` pointer. The `next` pointer points to an item of the same type as the `struct` itself, namely `listitem`. It is my intention to create a list of `structs` with each `struct` containing an integer value and a pointer to the next element – the next `struct` – in the list.

I create two pointer variables, `listhead` and `temp`. At the start, I set `listhead` to `NULL`. To help show what's going on here, I'm going to draw some diagrams. The first diagram is extremely simple. It just shows the value of the `listhead` pointer which is `NULL`:

LISTITEM or listitem?

The `next` pointer defined within the `LISTITEM struct` is declared as a pointer to `listitem` rather than to `LISTITEM`. That's because the `LISTITEM` (uppercase) hasn't been declared yet – it's declared at the end of the `typedef`. So you can't just declare `next` using the `LISTITEM` type as I've declared the two pointers in `main()`. The compiler *may* allow you to declare `next` by preceding `LISTITEM` with the `struct` keyword as `struct LISTITEM *next` – but logically it should be declared as `struct listitem *next` which is what I have done here.

First Turn Through the Loop

I execute this `for` loop to create and initialize three `listitem` structs, allocating the correct amount of memory for each, using `malloc()`. I initialize the `data` field of each `struct` with an integer from 0 to 2. And then I set its `next` pointer to point to the `listhead` pointer:

```
for (int i = 0; i < 3; i++) {
    temp = (LISTITEM*)malloc(sizeof(LISTITEM));
    temp->data = i;
    temp->next = listhead;
    listhead = temp;
}
```

After the first turn through the loop (when `i` is `0`) my new pointer, `temp`, points to a `struct` whose `data` is `0`, and whose `next` pointer points to the `listhead` pointer which is `NULL`. So we have this:

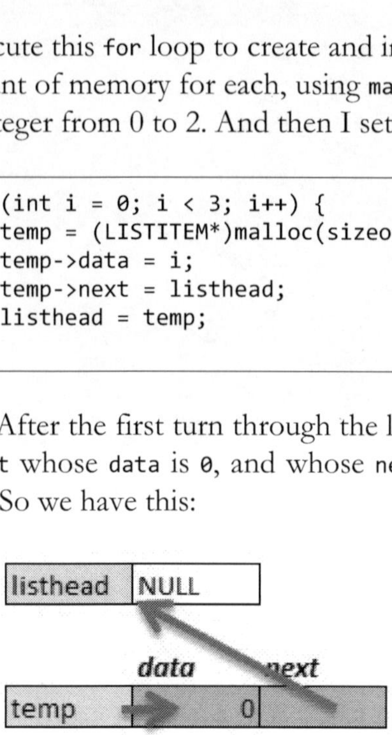

The final line of code in the loop assigns `temp` to the `listhead` pointer. So now `listhead` points to the new `struct`:

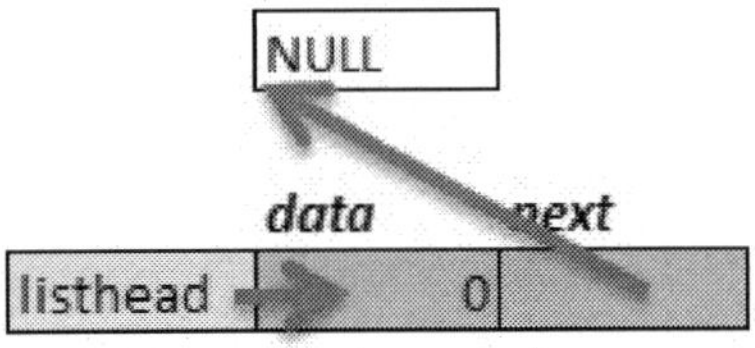

Next Turn Through the Loop

After the next turn through the loop (`i` is now `1`), another `struct` is created and its `data` field is assigned the value 1. Its `next` pointer once again points to `listhead`. So this is now the situation:

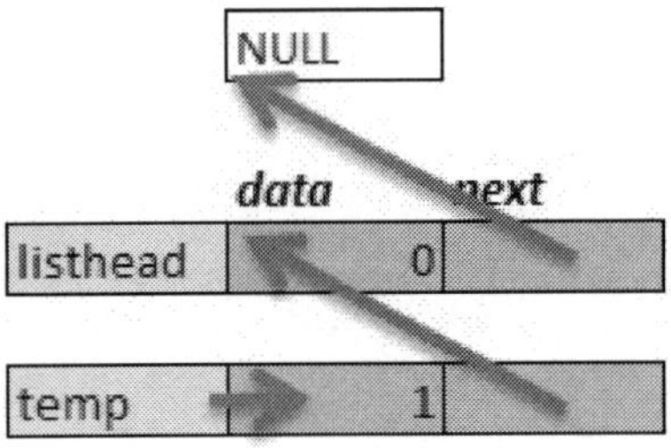

And, as before, the `listhead` pointer is updated to point to the newly created `struct`:

```
listhead = temp;
```

So this is how things stand now, on the second turn through the `for` loop: the `listhead` pointer now points to the `struct` containing the `data` 1 and a pointer `next` which points to the `struct` containing the data 0 and a pointer `next` which points to `NULL`.

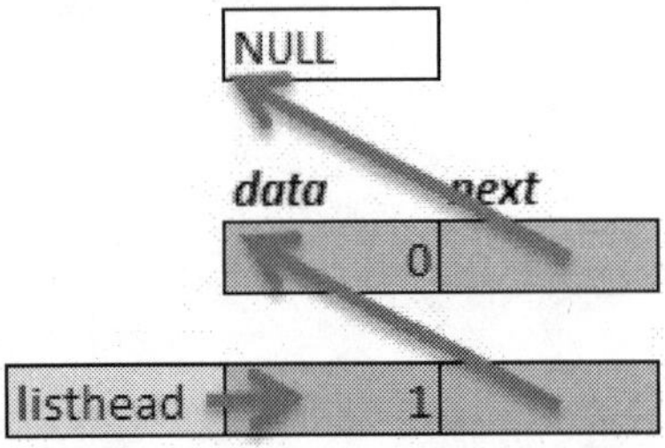

And So On

The same thing is repeated on the third turn through the loop. So then we end up with something like this:

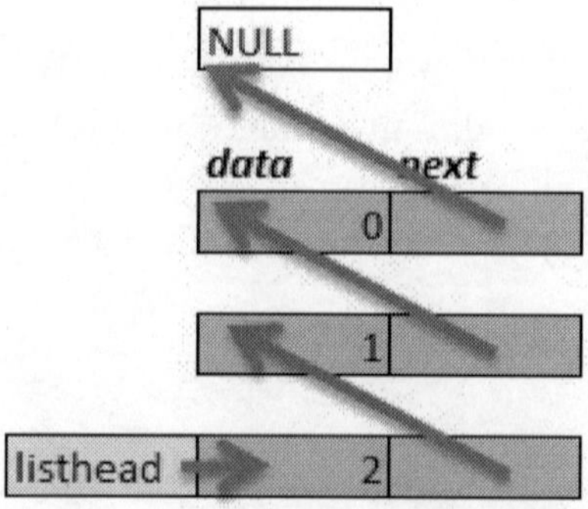

The `listhead` pointer now points to the last `struct` we added, whose `data` field is 2. Its `next` field, which is a pointer, points to the previous `struct` we added, whose `data` field is 1. The `next` pointer of *this* `struct` points to yet another `struct` whose `data` is 0. And *its* `next` pointer points to `NULL`, which is the end of the list.

When I run the program, I execute this `while` loop to trace through the list:

```
while (temp != NULL) {
    printf("list item: \n\tcurrent is %p\n\t next is %p\n\tdata is %d\n",
           temp,temp->next, temp->data);
    temp = temp->next;
}
```

This traces back from the last item I added, which is at the head of the list, right back to the first item I added. You can see that each `next` pointer points to the address of the preceding `struct` in the list until I arrive at the end of the list when `next` points to `NULL` (that is: `00000000`):

```
list item:
        current is 009C53F8
        next is 009C5A30
        data is 2
list item:
        current is 009C5A30
        next is 009C59F8
        data is 1
list item:
        current is 009C59F8
        next is 00000000
        data is 0
```

To free or not to free?

In the *SingleLinkedList* program, no attempt is made to free any of the allocated memory. You often don't need to free memory in programs where memory that is allocated remains in use – that is, it remains referenced by pointers – throughout the entire lifetime of the program.

When you close the program, any allocated memory will be automatically freed. At least it will on a desktop operating system. Even so, we do need to know how to free memory from list items explicitly and I'll look at that later on.

Doubly-linked Lists

A singly-linked list lets you move from one element to the next but, in so doing, you immediately lose track of the previous element because there is no link back to it.

It is sometimes useful to be able to move either way in a list. For example, imagine that you created a list to contain records, structs, of some sort – a list of employees, a list of the books in a library or of the treasures in a game.

A doubly-linked list not only has a pointer to the next element, but also to the previous element. This makes it just as easy to move in either direction through the list.

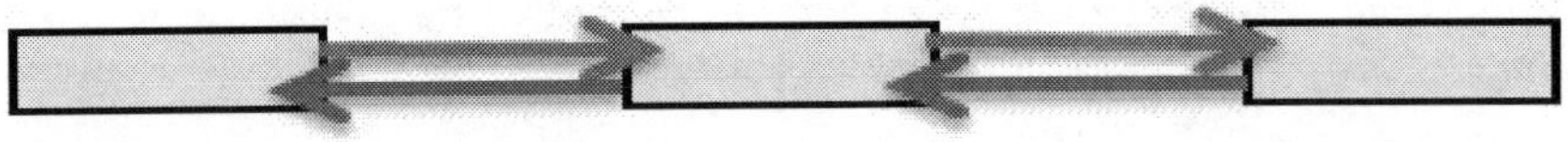

So if you want to delete some records at the end of the list (for example) you can easily backtrack through records from that end in a doubly-linked list rather than having to work your way from the start of the list as you would have to do with a singly-linked list.

Programming a Doubly-linked List

In this first example I create a very simple doubly-linked list.

DoublyLinkedList

```
typedef struct listitem {
    struct listitem *next;              // pointer to next item
    struct listitem *prev;              // pointer to previous item
    int data;                           // some data
} LISTITEM;

typedef struct {
    struct listitem *first;             // pointer to first item
    struct listitem *last;              // pointer to last item
} LIST;

LIST list;                              // our list

int main() {
    LISTITEM *temp;

    list.first = (LISTITEM*)&list;
    list.last = (LISTITEM*)&list;

    for (int i = 0; i < 3; i++) {
        temp = (LISTITEM*)malloc(sizeof(LISTITEM));
        temp->data = i;
        temp->next = list.first;
        list.first = temp;
        temp->prev = (LISTITEM*)&list;
        temp->next->prev = temp;
    }

    temp = list.first;
    while (temp != (LISTITEM*)&list) {
        printf("forward list item: current is %p; next is %p; prev is %p; data \
is %d\n", temp, temp->next, temp->prev, temp->data);
        temp = temp->next;
    }
    temp = list.last;
    while (temp != (LISTITEM*)&list) {
        printf("backward list item: current is %p; next is %p; prev is %p; data \
is %d\n", temp, temp->next, temp->prev, temp->data);
        temp = temp->prev;
    }
    return 0;
}
```

The LISTITEM struct

I start by defining a `struct` to hold some data – here that's just an `int` but it could be any sort of data with multiple data fields in each `struct`:

```
typedef struct listitem {
    int data;
} LISTITEM;
```

Then, I declare two pointers to a `struct` of this same type. These pointers are fields of the `struct` itself. One (`next`) points to the next `struct` in a list, another (`prev`) points to the previous `struct`. So this is the finished version of the `LISTITEM struct`:

```
typedef struct listitem {
    struct listitem *next;     // pointer to next item
    struct listitem *prev;     // pointer to previous item
    int data;                  // some data
} LISTITEM;
```

The LIST struct

I have defined another `struct` called `LIST` to keep track of the first and last items in the list. The two pointers of the `LIST struct` have been given the names `first` and `last`. These two pointers will let us quickly get at the elements at both ends of the list:

```
typedef struct {
    struct listitem *first;
    struct listitem *last;
} LIST;
```

It is common practice when manipulating lists to keep track of the first element and the last element in that list. You could do that by defining two standalone pointer variables – a *headpointer* and a *tailpointer* – to point to the first and last elements. If the list is changed (as elements are added or deleted at start or end of the list), then those two variables would be updated accordingly.

Instead of having two unrelated pointers, it is neater to put the *headpointer* and *tailpointer* variables into a special 'list-management' structure. That's what I've done here.

I've declared two variables, `temp` and `list`.

`temp` is a *pointer* to a `LISTITEM struct`:

```
LISTITEM *temp;
```

`list` *is* a `LIST struct` – *not* a pointer to a `LIST struct`:

```
LIST list;
```

Keep in mind the `list struct` is a special 'stand-alone' `LIST` structure that is used to keep track of the start and end elements in a list. The `list struct` is *not* an element of the list itself. List elements are defined by the `LISTITEM struct` and each item only 'knows about' the element 'adjacent to' it (pointed to by the `next` or `prev` pointers).

But `list` is defined by the `LIST struct`. It knows about the start and the end of the list (the items pointed to by the `first` and `last` pointers). If you wanted to keep any other information about the list (for example, its size), you could add additional fields to the `LIST struct`.

Here I initialize the `list struct` by setting both its `first` pointer and its `last` pointers to point to the `list struct` itself – that is, they are assigned the address of `list`:

```
list.first = (LISTITEM*)&list;
list.last = (LISTITEM*)&list;
```

This is the situation we now have: a `list struct` that contains `first` and `last` pointers, both of which point to the `list struct`.

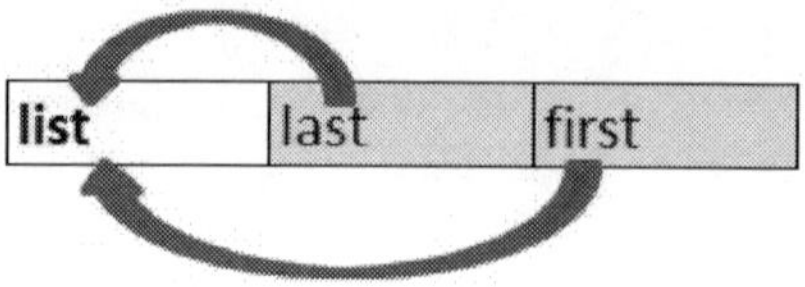

I could have decided to set the `first` and `last` pointers to `NULL` but I prefer to make them point to something valid – here the `struct` which contains the pointers themselves.

Notice that I have cast `&list` to a pointer to `LISTITEM`:

```
(LISTITEM*)&list;
```

That's because the first and last pointers are defined to be pointers to listitem. However, when these pointers don't point to an item in the list, I deliberately make them point to the list management struct which is a LIST, not a LISTITEM. This is correct, and it is what I intend to do, but even so the compiler may think it's a mistake. I need the cast to tell the compiler that this really is my intention, so that it doesn't display error or warning messages.

Memory allocation

When I declare a *pointer* to a struct (like *temp) I have to allocate memory for it. But when I declare a simple struct (like list) I don't. That's because the C compiler knows the exact size and location in memory of a simple struct variable when the program is compiled and run so it can allocate sufficient memory for it. With *pointers* to structs, new structs can be created and deleted during the execution of the program. These may come and go at runtime, so the memory needed is not known and can't be allocated in advance.

This for loop creates some structs. It allocates memory and initialises the data field for each of them:

```
for (int i = 0; i < 3; i++) {
    temp = (LISTITEM*)malloc(sizeof(LISTITEM));
    temp->data = i;
    temp->next = list.first;
    list.first = temp;
    temp->prev = (LISTITEM*)&list;
    temp->next->prev = temp;
}
```

Look how it deals with the pointers. Even at first sight, you can see that this is quite a bit more complicated than the code we used to wire up the elements in a singly-linked list.

In fact, if this is the first time you've ever used a doubly-linked list, the chances are you will need to stare at this code, and run it, maybe using your debugger, before you can even begin to understand what is going on here.

Let me help you. Shortly, I will go through this code in minute detail. First, however, let me explain one of the problems you have to solve when creating doubly-linked lists.

Constructing a Doubly-linked List

Constructing a doubly-linked list is a bit trickier than constructing a singly-linked list. When I created a *singly*-linked list I just kept adding structs at the front of the existing list.

Here's my *singly*-linked list…

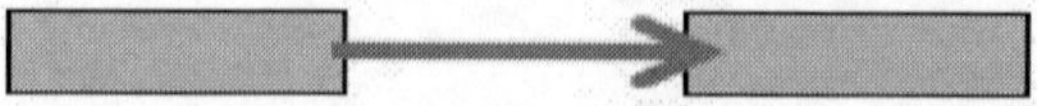

Now I add a new `struct` and set a pointer to the `struct` that was previously at the end of the list.

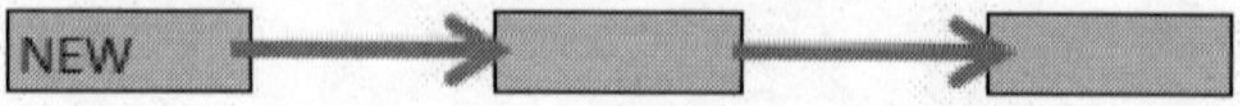

But with a *doubly*-linked list, I need pointers to point in *both* directions – that is, both to the *previous* element in the list and to the *next* element.

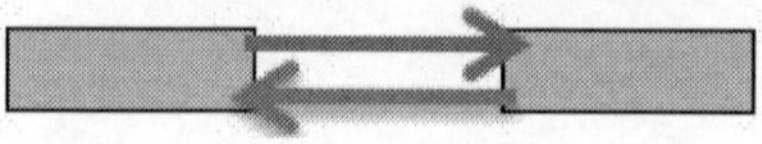

This poses an interesting problem. When I add a `struct` I can set its pointer to the `struct` on one side of it – that is, to the previously added `struct`.

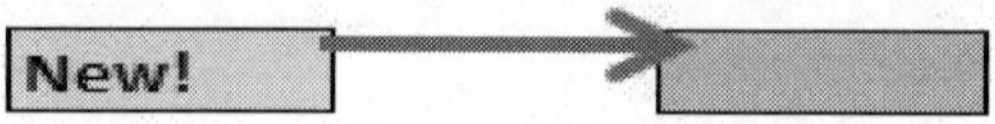

But I can't set a pointer to the `struct` on the other side –because I haven't added that `struct` yet.

Let's see how we can deal with this problem.

Implementing a Doubly-linked List

Now let's get back to the code and go through the process of creating forward and backward links. You may want to refer back to the code of the *DoublyLinkedList* sample program which I showed earlier on. Better still, load the code supplied in the code archive into your C editor or IDE.

list – the 'List Management' struct

As explained earlier, this program uses a `list` structure which has pointers that will point to the first and last elements in my list. But `list` itself is not in the list. It stands separate from the list and uses its `first` and `last` pointers to point to structs at the two ends of the list. Initially the `first` and `last` pointers of `list` go nowhere – they just point back to the `list` struct itself.

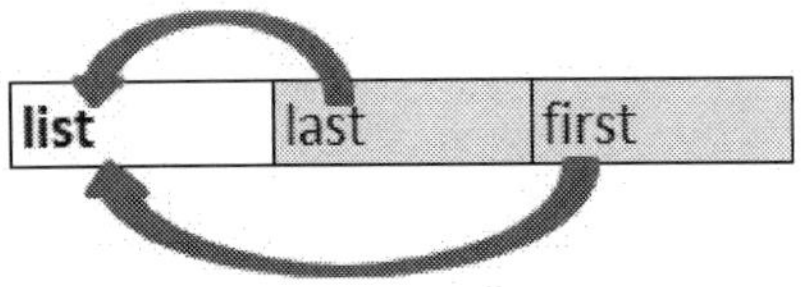

An empty list?

The `list struct` contains pointers, `first` and `last`, which are intended to point to the `LISTITEM` elements at the start and end of a doubly-linked list. When there are no list elements, the list is 'empty'. Even so, the `first` and `last` pointers need to point somewhere. In my program when the list is empty, I indicate this by making these two pointers point to the `list struct`.

Now I create the list:

```
for (int i = 0; i < 3; i++) {
    temp = (LISTITEM*)malloc(sizeof(LISTITEM));
    temp->data = i;
    temp->next = list.first;
    list.first = temp;
    temp->prev = (LISTITEM*)&list;
    temp->next->prev = temp;
}
```

When creating a new `LISTITEM struct`, I use the `temp` variable. First of all, I add some data (`temp->data = i`) and then I assign `list.first` to the `next` pointer of `temp`:

```
temp->next = list.first;
```

This has the effect of making `temp->next` point to the `list struct` because, that's where the `list.first` pointer points at the moment:

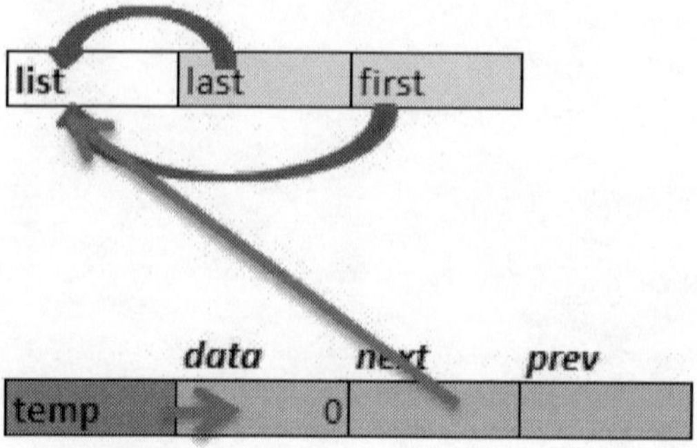

Then I make the `list.first` pointer point to `temp`:

```
list.first = temp;
```

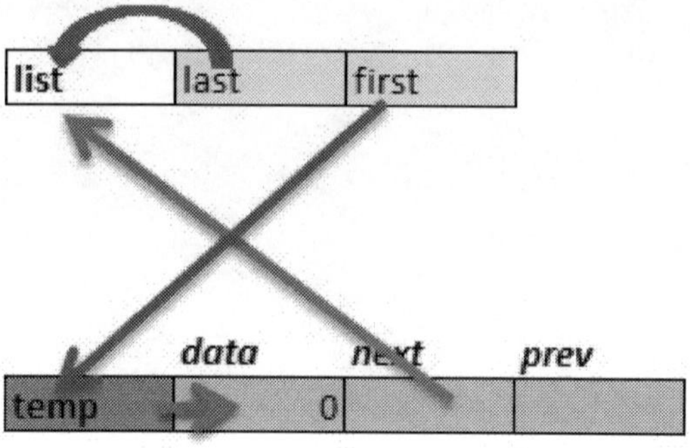

Which is first, which is last?

There isn't really a start and an end of a doubly-linked list. Since links go in both directions, all we can really say is that the list has two ends. However, it is convenient to think of the list 'starting' at one end (with a 'first' element) and 'ending' at the other (with a 'last' element).

I make the `temp->prev` pointer point to `list` (I have to use a cast because a `LIST` isn't the same as a `LISTITEM`, but I do want the *address* of `list` to be used):

```
temp->prev = (LISTITEM*)&list;
```

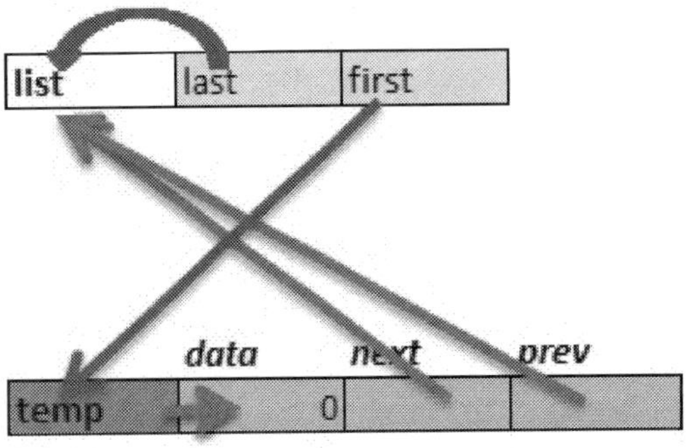

And now comes the really tricky bit:

```
temp->next->prev = temp;
```

Here I use the `temp->next` pointer to get at the next element and I set the `prev` pointer *of that element* to point to `temp`. Let's look at this carefully: `temp->next` currently points to `list`. That means that `temp->next->prev` is the same as `list.last` (see the note on the next page for an explanation of this). So here I am assigning `temp` to `list.last`. This is now the situation:

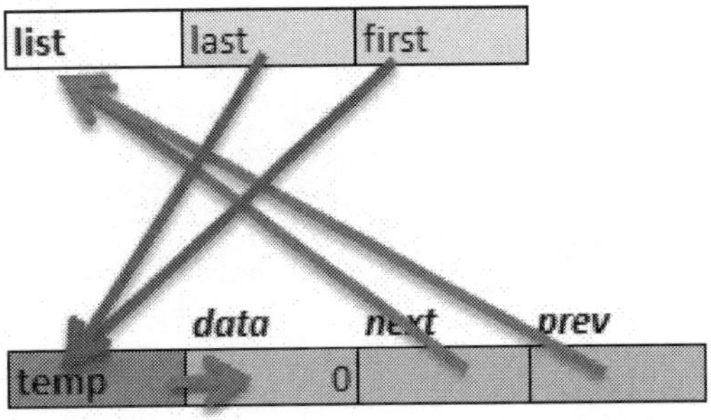

At this point I have just one element in my list. Both its `next` and `prev` pointers point to a special `struct` called `list` that keeps track of the start and end of the list. But as there is only one element in the list, `list.last` and `list.first` both point to the same list element.

Now let's see what happens when we add another element. I first create a new `struct` to assign to `temp`:

```
temp = (LISTITEM*)malloc(sizeof(LISTITEM));
```

The `data` field of this new `temp struct` is assigned the integer 1 because the loop variable `i` is 1:

```
temp->data = i;
```

The code then makes this assignment:

```
temp->next = list.first;
```

Currently `list.first` points to the previously added element in the list (see the previous diagram). So the assignment `temp->next = list.first` causes the `temp->next` pointer to point to the previously added element.

temp->next->prev?

I just said that when I assigned temp to `temp->next->prev` I actually ended up assigning temp to `list.last`? But how can that be? Surely I assigned temp to a pointer called prev, not to one called `last`. Well, in fact, it's not quite that straightforward. Let me explain.

I have defined the a `LIST struct` with two pointer fields that have the same 'layout' as the two pointer fields of a `LISTITEM struct`:

```
typedef struct listitem {
    struct listitem *next;
    struct listitem *prev;
    int data;
} LISTITEM;

typedef struct {
    struct listitem *first;
    struct listitem *last;
} LIST;
```

Those fields are 'compatible'. They are both pointers to `listitem` and they occupy the same 'positions' within the `struct`. They are 'aligned' on the same boundaries. Refer back to the explanation of data-type alignment in Chapter 6 if you need a quick refresher on data alignment.

This is the situation now:

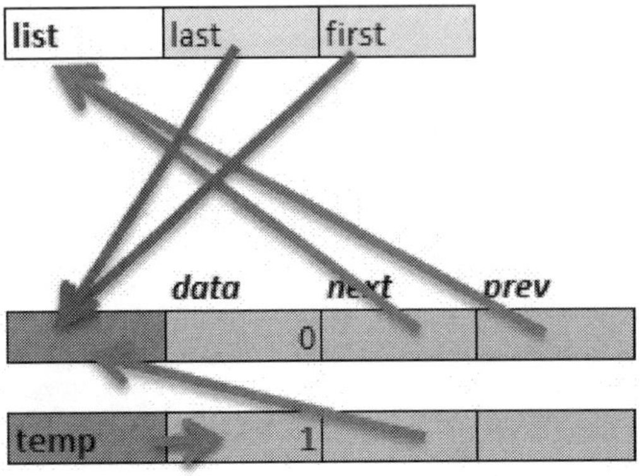

The `list.first` pointer is set to point to the new `struct`, `temp`:

```
list.first = temp;
```

So now `list.last` points to the previously-added element and `list.first` points to the newly-added element:

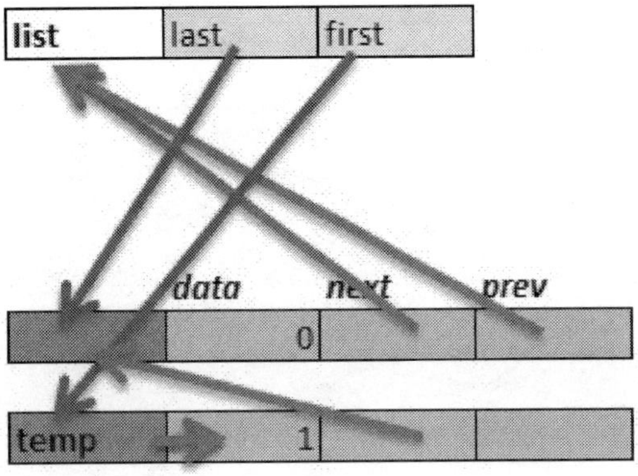

The `temp->prev` pointer is set to point to `list`:

```
temp->prev = (LISTITEM*)&list;
```

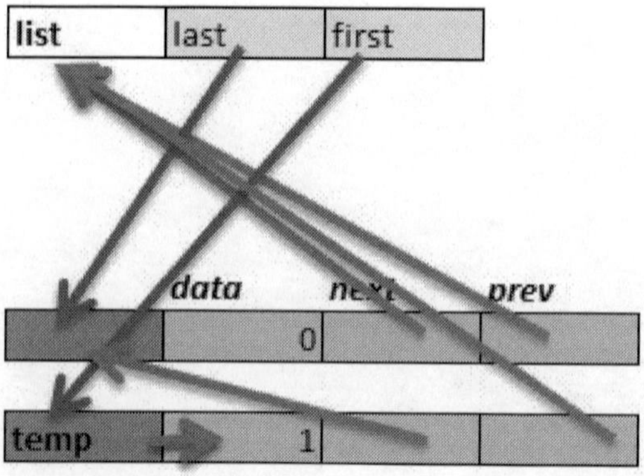

Then finally we get to this complicated assignment again:

```
temp->next->prev = temp;
```

Let's work that out. Looking back at the last diagram, I can see that `temp->next` points to the `struct` (with `data` item 0) that we previously added to the list. I've called this pointer `next` because I'm treating the most recently added structure as the start of my list, so the item that was added immediately before it is the next element to it. In my diagram, that's the one with data equal to 0. I'll call it *Element 0*.

That means that when my code makes an assignment to `temp->next->prev`, the assignment is actually made to the `prev` pointer of *Element 0*. The `prev` pointer of *Element 0* is now set to point to `temp`:

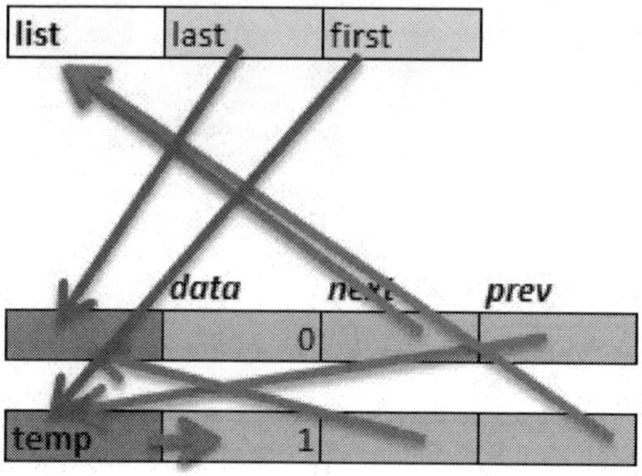

The `prev` pointer of the newly added `struct` always points back to the `list struct`. That indicates that this newly-added `struct` is at one end of the list because its `prev` pointer does not point to another (previous) list element. However, its `next` pointer does point to another element.

This may still seem a bit confusing at the moment but if I add another `struct` to the list you will see that there is a pattern. This is the situation when we add a third `struct`:

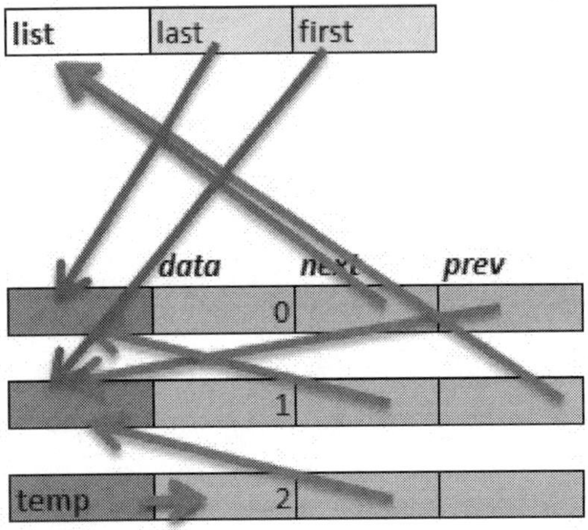

This time its `data` is 2. Its `next` pointer is assigned `list.first` which currently points to the previously added `struct`. Then `list.first` is set to point to this new `struct`. And `temp->prev` is set to point to `list`. This is now how all the pointers are connected up:

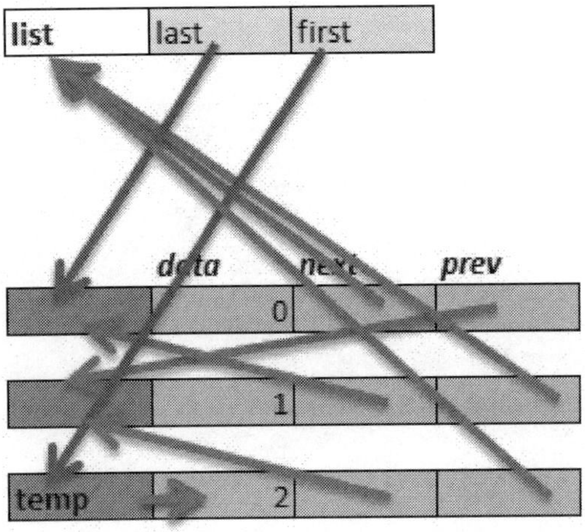

Finally this:

```
temp->next->prev = temp;
```

Let's see: `temp->next` points to the previous `struct` in the list. So we are setting *its* `prev` pointer to point to the newly added `struct`, like this:

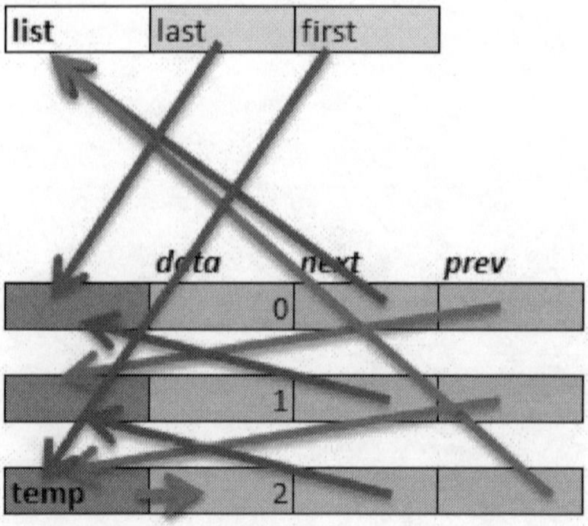

Can you see that every time a new `struct` is added, its `next` pointer points to the `struct` that was added before it in the list? Its `prev` pointer points to the `struct` added after it in the list.

For simplicity, we can think of the most recently added item here – the one that contains the `int` 2 – as being the start or the head of the list. The first item – the one that contains 0 – we can think of as being the end or the tail of the list.

So starting with the `struct` containing 2, I can use its `next` pointer to get to the `struct` the containing 1. And then I can use *its* `next` pointer to the `struct` containing 0. *Its* `next` pointer points to the `list struct` so I know I've come to the end of the list.

To go *backward* through the list, I start with the `struct` whose `data` is 0 and use the `prev` pointers to move through the list elements in the opposite direction – until once again I arrive at a pointer to `list`. And that's the end of the list.

When I run the *DoublyLinkedList* program, this is what I see:

```
forward list item: current is 01037868; next is 01028940;
     prev is 00DEFB08; data is 2
forward list item: current is 01028940; next is 01028840;
     prev is 01037868; data is 1
forward list item: current is 01028840; next is 00DEFB08;
     prev is 01028940; data is 0
backward list item: current is 01028840; next is 00DEFB08;
     prev is 01028940; data is 0
backward list item: current is 01028940; next is 01028840;
     prev is 01037868; data is 1
backward list item: current is 01037868; next is 01028940;
     prev is 00DEFB08; data is 2
```

This shows that when I trace 'forward' I start with the `struct` whose `data` is 2 and I use the `next` pointers to traverse the list in one direction:

```
temp = list.first;
while (temp != (LISTITEM*)&list) {
        // printf() here
    temp = temp->next;
}
```

And when I go 'backward' I start with the `struct` containing 0 and use the `prev` pointers to traverse the list in the other direction:

```
temp = list.last
while (temp != (LISTITEM*)&list) {
        // printf() here
    temp = temp->prev;
}
```

I can easily find the `struct` at either end of the list since the `list.first` pointer points to one end and the `list.last` pointer points to the other end.

As mentioned earlier, a doubly-linked list doesn't really have a start and end or 'first' and 'last' elements. It's worth emphasising this. Because, unlike a linear array, a doubly-linked list does not have an intrinsic sequential order.

If you like, you could treat the `struct` containing 0, as the start of the list and the one containing 2, as the end. But there is really no first or last element as they are all linked to one another in *both* directions and the list can be traversed in *either* direction. When we talk about the start and the end, or when we name pointers `first`, `last`, `next` and `prev`, this is just because it makes it easier for us to keep track of what is going on. You could rename the pointer variables and the code would work just the same.

Now we know how to create a doubly-linked list, we need to find out how we can actually use it. For that we'll examine two common data-structures: the queue and the stack.

8 – Queues and Stacks

Queues are very common data structures in programming so you need to understand exactly what they are.

A Queue is First-In, First-Out

A queue is a list in which the first thing you add is also the first thing that you remove. In other words, if I create a list from A to Z. I would build the list by adding A first and Z last. When I want to remove an item from the queue, I take A first, then, B, C, D and so on. This is called First-In, First-Out or FIFO.

Queues are typically used when you want to deal with things in a time-based order. The things that are added to the queue early on have *higher priority* than the things that are added later. That's the way, for example, that your computer handles a printer queue. You add document 1, then document 2, then document 3 to the queue. And the printer prints them in that order. The first thing you added, document 1, is the first thing that gets printed. In that sense, it has a higher priority than things that were added after it.

Queues are Everywhere!

Queues are very common data structures in programming. Think of the operating system's event queue. This is the queue that keeps track of keyboard or mouse events. A mouse-move or a mouse-click event is put onto the end of the event-queue where it waits until the operating system has time to process it. It has to wait until all the events *before* it in the queue are processed.

When all the events before it have been processed, the mouse event is pulled off the queue and sent to the program. That ensures that mouse events are processed in the correct order so that, for example, if you clicked the left-mouse button to select a cell in a spreadsheet and you then made a series of mouse moves – each of which generates a mouse-move event – those events are processed in the right order. If they weren't – if for example, the mouse-move events were processed *before* the mouse-click – you wouldn't end up selecting cells as you intended.

Similarly if keyboard events weren't processed in the order in which keys were pressed you would never be able to write meaningful sentences in a word processor because the characters would appear in a different order than when entered on the keyboard. A queue ensures that the correct order is maintained so your spreadsheet and word processor work as intended.

Queues as Doubly-linked Lists

In this next example, I've adapted my doubly-linked list so that I can use it as a queue. There are other ways of programming queues but this is a convenient way of doing it. As before, `LISTITEM` defines list elements; `LIST` is the 'list manager' that keeps track of the first and last elements in the queue:

Queue

```
typedef struct listitem {
    struct listitem *next;
    struct listitem *prev;
    int data;
} LISTITEM;

typedef struct {
    struct listitem *first;
    struct listitem *last;
} LIST;

LIST list;
```

The two really important new features of this code are the `enqueue()` and `dequeue()` functions. The `enqueue()` function is used to add a new item to the back of the queue; `dequeue()` is used to remove an item from the front of the queue:

```
void enqueue(LISTITEM *item) {
    LISTITEM *temp;
    temp = list.last;
    list.last = item;
    item->prev = temp;
    item->next = (LISTITEM*)&list;
    temp->next = item;
}

LISTITEM *dequeue() {
    LISTITEM *temp;
    temp = list.first;
    if (temp == (LISTITEM*)&list) {
        temp = NULL;
    } else {
        list.first = temp->next;
        list.first->prev = (LISTITEM*)&list;
    }
    return temp;
}
```

Think of the queue like this.

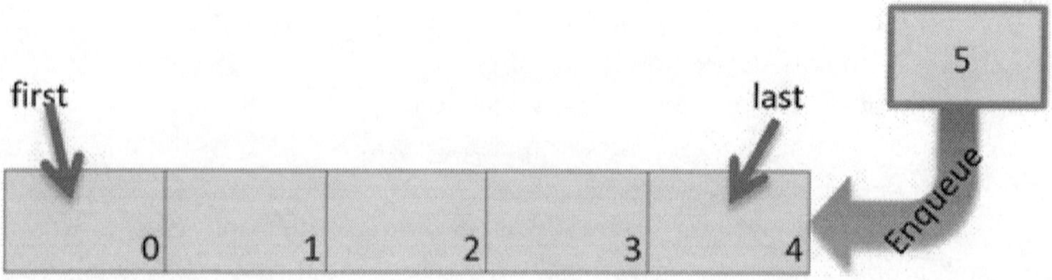

The queue itself is a list of elements – and I keep pointers to the first element and the last element in the list.

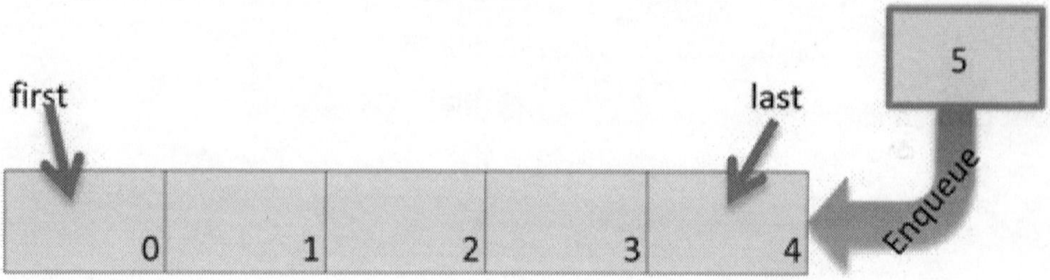

When I have a new item that I want to add to the list (here that's *Element 5*). I add it to the end of the queue. That is called enqueueing. This now becomes the last element.

When I want to take an item from the list I take the first item. The item at the start of the queue (here that's *Element 0*). That is called dequeueing.

This is a bit like a line of people waiting to go into a cinema.

Person 0 is the first to arrive so Person 0 is at the beginning of the line, that is at the beginning of the queue.

Person 4 is the last to arrive and so Person 4 goes to the end of the queue. When another person arrives, Person 5, then Person 5 goes to the end of the queue.

When the doors are opened and people start to go into the cinema, the person at the beginning of the queue, Person 0, goes first…

In programming jargon, Person 0 is dequeued.

Meanwhile, another person, Person 6, arrives and is added to the end of the queue. In the jargon, Person 6 is enqueued.

I don't plan to go over the code of this program in the same minute detail as when I explained doubly-linked lists. If you followed that tutorial carefully, you should be able to work out what is going on by loading and running the *Queue* project yourself. Take time to look at the `enqueue()` function. That goes to the end of the list – with the help of the `list.last` pointer:

```
temp = list.last;
```

It adds a new item (here `item` is a pointer to a `LISTITEM`) the end of the list:

```
list.last = item;
```

It assigns the new item's `prev` pointer to `temp` (that is `list.last`) which is the previous element in the queue and its `next` pointer to `list`. The end result is that the new item is put at the back of the queue:

```
item->prev = temp;
item->next = (LISTITEM*)&list;
```

And finally I reset the `next` pointer of `temp` to point to the newly added item. At the moment temp is pointing to the item that *was* the final item of the queue (`list.last`) *before* I added the new item:

```
temp->next = item;
```

The `dequeue()` function does exactly the opposite. It gets the element at the front of the queue, using `list.first`, removes it, returns it, and adjusts the pointers so that the new `list.first` pointer to points to the new first item (that is, the one following the item that has just been dequeued).

In the `main()` function, the element that was returned by `dequeue()` is tested to ensure that it is a valid `struct`. Here it will be `NULL` if it isn't, because that is what `dequeue()` will return in that case, that is if there is nothing left in the queue. If the `struct` is not `NULL` I just print out its data and then free its memory:

```
temp = dequeue();
if (temp != NULL) {
    printf("data is %d\n", temp->data);
    free(temp);
}
```

When I run it you can see the result.

```
first item = 0
last item = 2

data is 0
data is 1
data is 2
```

The queue is created – enqueued - with the `struct` containing 0 first and the `struct` containing 2 last. And when it's dequeued, that order is maintained. The first in, 0, is the first out, then 1, then 2.

A Stack is Last-In, First Out

A stack is another very important type of data structure. Whereas a queue is a First-In-First-Out structure (where the first thing that's added to the queue is also the first thing that's taken off the queue), a stack, is a Last-In-First-Out structure. The last thing – that is the thing most recently added to the stack – is the first thing that's taken off it.

Stack vs queue

Queue = *First-In-First-Out* (FIFO). You can think of a queue as a bit like a line of people waiting to go to the cinema. First come, first served. The first to join the queue is also the first to leave the queue.

Stack = *Last-In-First-Out* (LIFO). But a stack is like a stack of plates. The last thing to be added in the stack, the plate right at the top, is the first to be taken off the stack (when I'm ready for my dinner).

Implementing a Stack

While a stack could be implemented as a linked list, that's not really necessary. In fact, unlike a queue or any type of linked list, a stack is typically declared to be of a fixed size. If you have a fixed size stack and you want to increase its size you would need to allocate a new block of memory and copy the existing stack elements into it. But for the sake of simplicity I'm not going to do that.

We've already seen other data structures – linked lists and queues – whose size can be increased easily. But with this example of a stack, I'm going to assume that you will set a maximum stack size and that won't be changed.

Why is a stack of fixed size?

While you *could* create a stack that grows in size, allocating memory for new items as required, often it is more efficient to create a stack of fixed size because that is simply faster. Stacks are frequently used for speed-efficient operations and it is faster to add and delete items without allocating memory for each item and 'wiring up' links between the items stored in the stack.

Stack

```
typedef struct {
    int a;
    double b;
} DATA;

DATA *base;
DATA *end;
DATA *top;

#define STACKSIZE 5

int push(DATA *data) {
    int ok;

    if (top == end) {          // any more room?
        ok = 0;                // no, so tell the caller
    } else {
        memcpy(top, data, sizeof(DATA));
        top = top + 1;
        ok = 1;
    }
    return ok;
}
DATA *pop() {
    DATA *data;

    if (top == base) {         // empty stack
        data = NULL;
    } else {
        top = top - 1;         // get the top item
        data = top;            // and return it
    }
    return data;
}
```

Stack (continued)

```
int main() {
    DATA data, *pdata;

    base = (DATA*)malloc(STACKSIZE * sizeof(DATA));
    end = base + STACKSIZE;
    top = base;

    // add data items to the stack until the stack memory is exhausted
    for (int i = 0; ; i++) {
        data.a = i;
        data.b = i * 2;
        if (!push(&data)) {
            break;
        }
    }

    printf("first item = %d : %f\n", base->a, base->b);
    pdata = base + 4;           // count 4 items up from the 1st struct (at base)
    printf("last item = %d : %f\n\n", pdata->a, pdata->b);

    do {
        pdata = pop();
        if (pdata != NULL)
            printf("data popped is %d : %f\n", pdata->a, pdata->b);
    } while (pdata != NULL);

    free(base);
    return 0;
}
```

My stack implementation is a sequential list of elements. There are no links between them; the elements do not have `next` or `prev` pointers to other elements as they did in my queue.

The stack occupies a single contiguous block of memory – that means that every item in the stack is stored in a piece of memory right next to the item immediately before it. In that respect it is like an array.

The stack is intended to contain a fixed number of items, each of a given size. Being quite a simple structure, a stack is faster to use than a queue. Also, as there are no pointers between the elements, a stack can contain any type of data item: it's not restricted to working with structs that contain pointers.

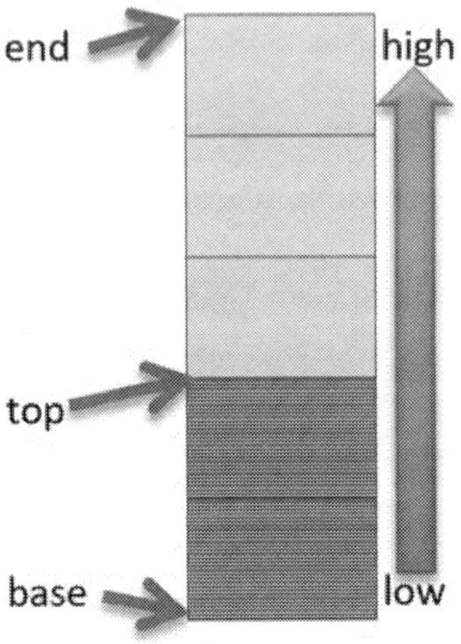

Let's consider how a stack is structured. In my program, the stack occupies a chunk of memory that starts at base – that is, at the address where my `base` pointer points – and ends at end where my `end` pointer points. I have a `top` pointer that is updated to point to the top item of the stack. The `top` pointer is updated when a new item is added.

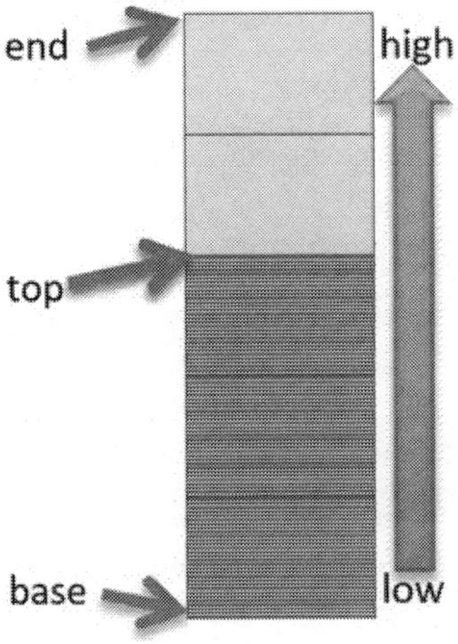

The stack grows in memory from the bottom upwards (from a low address to a higher address). That isn't necessarily the case. You can create a stack that grows downwards from a high address to a lower address. But my stack grows upwards just like a stack of plates as more plates are added onto it.

The call stack

The call stack is a special stack that is used to keep track of function calls, their arguments and any local variables. Most good C debuggers – such as the Visual Studio debugger – provide a tool to view the call stack. The 'call stack' is often referred to simply as 'the stack'.

Pushing and Popping

By tradition, when you add an item onto the top of a stack, it is said that you push it there. I've written a `push()` function that does that in my code:

```
int push(DATA *data) {
    int ok;

    if (top == end) {           // any more room?
        ok = 0;                 // no, so tell the caller
    } else {
        memcpy(top, data, sizeof(DATA));
        top = top + 1;
        ok = 1;
    }
    return ok;
}
```

I first check to see if the stack has room for another item. I do this by checking if `top` (my pointer to the top of the stack) equals `end`, which is the pointer to the end of the memory set aside to hold the stack.

These pointers have been assigned in `main()`:

```
base = (DATA*)malloc(STACKSIZE * sizeof(DATA));
end = base + STACKSIZE;
top = base;
```

The `base` pointer is where the memory for my stack begins. That's because `malloc()` returns a pointer to the start of the allocated memory. And `end` is a pointer to the end of the allocated memory – because it's the address of `base` plus `STACKSIZE` which is a constant I defined earlier and, here, it happens to be 5. And `top` – the top element in the stack is here the same as `base` as there isn't yet anything in the stack.

If the top of the stack has reached the end of allocated memory then there isn't any room for a new element. Otherwise, this code executes:

```
memcpy(top, data, sizeof(DATA));
top = top + 1;
ok = 1;
```

This uses `memcpy()` to copy the `data`, a new item, which here happens to be a `struct`, at the location of the top of the stack. It then increments the `top` pointer. This is another example of pointer arithmetic. My code increments `top` by the size of one element of the type to which `top` points – here that's a `DATA struct`.

When you take something off a stack you are usually said to pop it off. And that's what my `pop()` function does:

```
DATA *pop() {
    DATA *data;

    if (top == base) {          // empty stack
        data = NULL;
    } else {
        top = top - 1;          // get the top item
        data = top;             // and return it
    }
    return data;
}
```

The `pop()` function is the exact reverse of the `push()` function. It tests if `top` equals `base` – in which case there is nothing left to pop. It's an empty stack. Otherwise it decrements the `top` pointer and returns a pointer to the `data struct` to be removed.

In `main()` a `do...while` loop calls `pop()` for each data item in the stack. Its `pdata` variable is a pointer to a `DATA` item so that lets me get at the data fields: `a` and `b`:

```
do {
    pdata = pop();
    if (pdata != NULL) printf("data popped is %d : %f\n", pdata->a, pdata->b);
} while (pdata != NULL);
```

Be careful, however. When you pop an item off the stack that item's data is not deleted from memory. All that happens is that the pointer referencing the top item is moved up and down. It is this pointer that tells you where the last valid element in the stack occurs.

It would be quite possible to read data from memory areas anywhere in the stack structure – between the `base` and `end` pointers. But if you read data in a location *above* the `top` pointer that would be an error.

While creating and maintaining a stack in this way is, in some ways, simpler than creating and maintaining a linked list – because you have only three pointers to worry about – `base`, `end` and `top` – you still need to take great care when adding or 'pushing' new items onto the stack because you must be sure that there is enough memory for them. And when deleting or 'popping' them off the stack you must be careful to check there is a valid item to be deleted.

Freeing the Stack

Finally, notice that I don't try to free up memory on an element by element basis. Memory is allocated for the entire stack at the outset (here `STACKSIZE` is 5 so I allocate 5 times the amount of memory needed for a single `DATA struct`). And assign that to the `base` pointer:

```
base = (DATA*)malloc(STACKSIZE * sizeof(DATA));
```

When I finish with the stack I clean up by freeing `base` to deallocate the memory block *for the entire stack* in a single operation:

```
free(base);
```

Let's see this running.

```
first item = 0 : 0.000000
last item = 4 : 8.000000

data popped is 4 : 8.000000
data popped is 3 : 6.000000
data popped is 2 : 4.000000
data popped is 1 : 2.000000
data popped is 0 : 0.000000
```

Remember a stack is a Last-In, First-Out structure. Here you can see that the last item that was added – pushed onto the stack – is the `struct` containing the integer and floating point numbers 4 and 8.0 and when I pop the items off the stack that last item is the one that is removed first. And so on through the other items in the stack until we get to the first item that was added which contains 0 integer and floating point values.

Calculating the Length of a List

We've looked at various ways of creating lists and adding items to them. Let's now see how to do various other useful things with some lists. To begin with, we'll look at a way of counting the items in a list. Here I'll use a queue, which is a doubly-linked list. The function, `queue_length()` counts the elements in the list and returns an integer.

QueueLength

```
int queue_length(LIST *queue) {
    LISTITEM *temp;
    int length;

    temp = queue->first;             // get the 'first' item
    length = 0;                      // initialize the length
    do {
        if (temp == (LISTITEM*)queue) {
            temp = NULL;             // break out of do...while loop
            break;
        }
        temp = temp->next;           // get the next item in the queue
        length = length + 1;
    } while (temp != NULL);

    return length;
}
```

The function is called with a parameter named `queue` which is a pointer to a `LIST` `struct`. As in previous programs, `LIST` is a `struct` which contains pointers to the first and last elements in a list. I have declared a variable `list`, as the 'header' or 'list manager' whose job it is to keep track of the start and end of the queue:

```
typedef struct {
    struct listitem *first;
    struct listitem *last;
} LIST;

LIST list;
```

As in my other examples, when the list is empty, the pointers in `list` point to the `list struct` itself:

```
list.first = (LISTITEM*)&list;
list.last = (LISTITEM*)&list;
```

The address of `list` is passed to `queue_length()`:

```
queue_length(&list)
```

Pointer parameters

Look at the declaration of the parameter `queue` in the `queue_length()` function:

```
int queue_length(LIST *queue)
```

Clearly this shows that `queue` is a pointer to `LIST`. And yet my code doesn't pass a *pointer* to the function. It passes an *address*:

```
queue_length(&list)
```

It turns out that when a parameter is declared as a pointer, its value may be initialized either by passing a pointer or by passing an address. When a *pointer* is passed, the value of the pointer parameter is initialized with the value of the pointer argument. When an *address* is passed, the value of the pointer parameter is initialized with the address.

In `queue_length()` I declare a `temp` variable which is a pointer to `LISTITEM` and I assign to `temp` the `first` pointer in the `LIST struct` (the `struct` pointed to by `queue`):

```
temp = queue->first;
```

When the queue is empty, the `list` struct's pointers (remember that `queue` points to the `list struct`) will be pointing to the `list struct` itself. So my code tests to see if `temp` points to `list`. Since `temp` is a pointer to `LISTITEM`, not to `LIST`, I have had to cast `queue` to a pointer to `LISTITEM` when testing this. If `temp` *does* point to `list` then the queue is empty and the function exits:

```
if (temp == (LISTITEM*)queue) {
    temp = NULL;
    break;
}
```

The `length` variable was initialized to 0 earlier in the function, so if the queue is empty, 0 is the value that's returned. Otherwise, the code keeps moving through the elements in the queue using their `next` pointers and incrementing the `length` variable each time:

```
temp = temp->next;
length = length + 1;
```

When I get to the end of the queue, `temp` will be pointing to the `list struct` – I then set `temp` to `NULL` and that provides the end condition for the `do...while` loop:

```
while (temp != NULL);
```

The function then exits returning the value of the local variable `length`.

This simple way of iterating over the elements in a queue, or other types of linked list, can be used to do other things too – not just count them. It is a generic technique for iterating through list elements. It might be useful in all kinds of different places when you need to do some operation, or calculation, on all the elements of a list. For example, you may want to calculate a total of the values of a certain field in each `struct` in the list; or you may want to change the values of certain fields.

If you run the *QueueLength* program, this is what you will see:

```
At start, the length of the queue is 0
After initialization, the length of the queue is 3

The length of the queue is now 3
Dequeued item. Data is 0
The length of the queue is now 2
Dequeued item. Data is 1
The length of the queue is now 1
Dequeued item. Data is 2
The length of the queue is now 0
```

At the outset the queue is empty so its length is 0. Then I add three structs so its length is now 3. Then I dequeue, removing items one by one from the queue and displaying the new length which, as you would expect is initially 3 then 2, then 1 and finally, when no more items remain, 0.

Copying a List

Sometimes you may need to make a copy of a list. There are lots of ways of doing that. Some ways may be simpler, some ways may be more elegant, and some ways may be faster than others. Here I am aiming for simplicity and I will continue to use a queue.

Keep It Simple!

Bear in mind that the examples in this chapter are kept deliberately simple. There are many more ways of using lists to create much more complex data structures. This is not a book about data structures and algorithms, however, and my aim is to help you understand how to create and manipulate lists by adding and deleting items, iterating over lists of items and ensuring that list pointers all point to valid items. Once you understand all that, you can refer to books of algorithms in order to see how these techniques can also be used with numerous other data structures.

Since I have already implemented `enqueue()` and `dequeue()` functions I already have much of the work done. To make a copy of an existing list I can transfer the items from one list by dequeueing them and adding those items to another list by enqueueing them. In the *ListTransfer* program, I start by declaring my two queue `LIST` structs: `src` is the source queue, `dst` is the destination queue:

ListTransfer

```
LIST src;
LIST dst;
```

In `main()`, I initialize their `first` and `last` pointers to point to themselves, which is my way of showing that they start out as empty queues:

```
src.first = (LISTITEM*)&src;
src.last = (LISTITEM*)&src;
dst.first = (LISTITEM*)&dst;
dst.last = (LISTITEM*)&dst;
```

Then I add some elements to the source queue using `enqueue()` which is the same function as the one I used in previous examples:

```
for (int i = 0; i < 3; i++) {
    temp = (LISTITEM*)malloc(sizeof(LISTITEM));
    temp->data = i;
    enqueue(&src, temp);
}
```

Now, I run a `do...while` loop to dequeue the source queue, `src`. This returns a list element which I assign to `temp` at each turn through the loop. I build the new queue by passing the dequeued element, `temp`, to my `enqueue()` function, calling it with the `dst` (destination queue) `LIST struct`:

```
do {
    temp = dequeue(&src);
    if (temp != NULL) {
        printf("data is %d\n", temp->data);
        enqueue(&dst, temp);
    }
} while (temp != NULL);
```

When I pass `dst` as an argument to `enqueue()` I precede the variable name with the address-of `&` operator: `&dst`. So I am actually passing, not the `struct` itself but the *address* of the `dst struct`. As explained earlier, when an address is passed as an argument, the value of a matching pointer parameter, such as `queue`, will be initialized with that address:

```
void enqueue(LIST *queue, LISTITEM *item)
```

Finally, in these two loops I call `dequeue()` with the two queues and display the result. This shows me the items in the destination queue (the one into which they were copied). The source queue will be empty now so I don't even try to display its items:

```
printf("destination queue ...\n");
do {
    temp = dequeue(&dst);
    if (temp != NULL) {
        printf("destination data is %d\n", temp->data);
        free(temp);
    }
} while (temp != NULL);

printf("source queue ...\n");
temp = dequeue(&src);
if (temp == NULL) {
    printf("source queue is empty\n");
}
```

This is what I see:

```
building destination queue ...
data is 0
data is 1
data is 2
destination queue ...
destination data is 0
destination data is 1
destination data is 2
source queue ...
source queue is empty
```

This shows that the elements from the source queue were added to the destination queue and removed from the source queue, leaving the source queue empty at the end.

In this example, whenever I add items to the destination queue I delete them from the source queue. I dequeue the source – removing elements – and then enqueue the destination – adding elements.

If you want to keep the source queue intact so that you end up with two copies, you could simply iterate through the source queue, instead of dequeueing them. I did that in the previous example, *QueueLength*, where I iterated over items in order to count them.

But be careful if you do that. If you end up with two queues that point to the *same* elements and *one* queue deletes an element without informing the *other* queue that it has done so, you could create big problems for yourself. Because one queue will now contain elements that point to something that no longer exists. I'll have more to say about this problem when I explain deep and shallow copying in Chapter 10.

Removing an Element from Within a List

We've used stacks and queues to remove items from the start or end of a list. But how would you delete an item from the *middle* of a list?

Often when you add or delete items to and from a list you do so in strict sequential order. That is, you add or delete the item from one end of the list, then the next item and so on. With a queue, you add items at the end of the queue and take items from the front of the queue. With stacks you add items on the top and take them off the top as well.

But what happens if you want to delete an item from somewhere inside a list or at a specific index in the list? That's a bit more difficult because you need to deal with any pointers from the elements on either side of the deleted item.

Let's take an example. Here I have a list (or a small part of a longer list) in which Element 9 and Element 11 both point to Element 10. And Element 10 has pointers to both Element 9 and Element 11. Let's now suppose that I want to delete Element 10…

If I delete an element, such as Element 10, from the middle of a doubly-linked list, the pointers that previously pointed to it (here the pointers from Elements 9 and 11) will now point to some random bit of memory – where the deleted element *used* to be.

I need to make sure that deleting an item does not 'break the links' in the list. So I must be sure to 'rewire' the pointers in adjacent elements of the deleted item to make sure they point to valid elements in the list. Here, for example, it would make sense to have the pointers from Element 9 and Element 11 point to one another, like this:

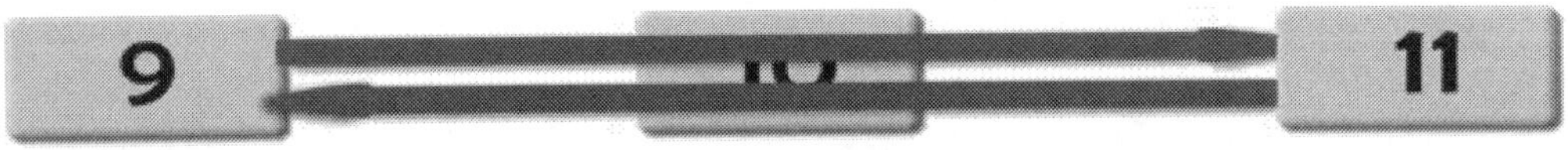

In the *RemoveAt* program, I build a list – in this case, containing five elements:

```
for (int i = 0; i < 5; i++) {
    temp = (LISTITEM*)malloc(sizeof(LISTITEM));
    temp->data = i;
    enqueue(&list, temp);
}
```

I ask the user to enter an index and then call the `remove_at()` function to try to delete the element at that index:

```
printf("enter the index of the queue entry ... ");
requested_index = atoi(gets(input));
temp = remove_at(&list, requested_index);
```

This is my remove_at() function:

RemoveAt

```
LISTITEM *remove_at(LIST *queue, int position) {
    LISTITEM *temp;
    int i;

    if (position < 0) {
        return NULL;
    }
    temp = queue->first;
    i = 0;
    do  {
            if (temp == (LISTITEM*)queue) {
            temp = NULL;
            break;
        }
        if (i == position) {
            temp->prev->next = temp->next;
            temp->next->prev = temp->prev;
            temp->next = NULL;
            temp->prev = NULL;
            break;
        }
        temp = temp->next;
        i = i + 1;
    } while (temp != NULL);
    return temp;
}
```

This gets the first item (temp = queue->first). Then, it iterates over the queue, up to the element at position which is the index that was entered by the user. It returns that element. If the returned element is not NULL (that is, if it is a valid element), it is freed in main():

```
temp = remove_at(&list, requested_index);
if (temp != NULL) {
    printf("OK: data removed at %d is %d\n", requested_index, temp->data);
    free(temp);
} else {
    printf("ERROR: cannot remove at %d\n", requested_index);
}
```

Finding an item at a specific index and freeing its memory is, as you can see, reasonably straightforward. But if my code happened to free its memory when the item was still a part of the list, that would cause problems – because, in effect, I would have broken the list structure. The previous and next items – the elements on either side of the one I've just removed – would still be trying to point to the removed element. Their `prev` and `next` pointer values would continue to be the address of an element that no longer exists.

Let's look how I deal with that problem.

When I locate the item to be removed, I have to have to 'rewire' the pointers on either side, so that the `next` pointer in the *previous* element points to whatever the element I am about to delete currently points to. That's what I do here:

```
temp->prev->next = temp->next;
```

And similarly, the `prev` pointer in the *next* element needs to point to whatever the `prev` pointer in the element I am removing currently points to. That's what I do here:

```
temp->next->prev = temp->prev;
```

And that's it. Once I have rewired the pointers from the elements on either side of the thing I'm about to remove, there is no longer anything in the list that points to it. By reassigning those pointers – so they continue to point to valid list elements – I've maintained the integrity of the list itself.

For neatness I now set the removed item's pointers to `NULL`:

```
temp->next = NULL;
temp->prev = NULL;
```

Setting the pointers of a deleted element to `NULL` is usually good practice. Though, in fact, in the present case it's not really necessary as I am about to free its memory anyway, and when I do that, this list element, the `temp struct`, will no longer exist.

Let's run this and see how it works.

```
the length of the queue is 5
enter the index of the queue entry ... 3
```

Here I have entered 3. The element at index 3 (the fourth element in this zero-based list) is deleted. But all other elements remain in the list.

```
OK: data removed at 3 is 3
the length of the queue is 4
data is 0
data is 1
data is 2
data is 4
```

If I enter 0, the first element is deleted. If I enter 4, the last element is deleted. If I enter an incorrect index, one that doesn't exist (here 10), nothing is removed but I see an error message.

```
the length of the queue is 5
enter the index of the queue entry ... 10
ERROR: cannot remove at 10
the length of the queue is 5
data is 0
data is 1
data is 2
data is 3
data is 4
```

Incidentally, if you want to remove *all* elements above a certain index, you can just put this code inside a loop:

```
do {
    temp = remove_at(&list, requested_index);
    if (temp != NULL) {
        printf("OK: data removed at %d is %d\n", requested_index, temp->data);
        free(temp);
    } else {
        printf("ERROR: cannot remove at %d\n", requested_index);
    }
} while (temp != NULL);
```

This time, I enter the index 3, the element at that index and at all higher indexes will be removed. First the matching item (index 3) is removed, the next item in the list becomes the new element at index 3. The loop executes again and so this element is also removed and so on to the end of the list – in this case until the 'error condition' occurs because there is no longer an element at index 3.

```
the length of the queue is 5
enter the index of the queue entry ... 3
OK: data removed at 3 is 3
OK: data removed at 3 is 4
ERROR: cannot remove at 3
the length of the queue is 3
data is 0
data is 1
data is 2
```

Adding an Element to a List

How would you add an item into a list? Of course, it's pretty straightforward to add an item onto the *end* of a list using a stack or queue. But how would you go about adding an item somewhere in the middle of a list?

That's what I do in my `add_after()` function:

AddAfter

```
LISTITEM *add_after(LIST *queue, int position, LISTITEM *item) {
    LISTITEM *temp;
    int i;

    if (position < 0) {
        return NULL;
    }
    temp = queue->first;
    i = 0;
    do {
        if (temp == (LISTITEM*)queue) {     // check for empty queue
            temp = NULL;
            break;
        }
        if (i == position) {                // code to insert new item
            item->next = temp->next;
            temp->next = item;
            item->prev = temp;
            item->next->prev = item;
            break;
        }
temp = temp->next;                          // get the next item in the queue
        i = i + 1;
    } while (temp != NULL);
    return temp;
}
```

Let's look at this.

In order to add an item you would need to make the pointers of the new item point to elements on either side of it. Say, if you wanted to add it after element 3, then it would need its `prev` and `next` pointers to point to elements 3 and 4.

And element 3 and 4 would need to have one each of their pointers set to point to the new item. Only by doing that will we be sure that the integrity of the list is preserved

– so that the next and prev pointers of the new item and the items on either side all point to the right things to ensure that the list items are all property joined up together.

In the add_after() function, given a position, an index into the queue, and a pointer to a new list element, item, I try to add the new item to the existing queue. This function needs to work with a queue that actually contains some elements so I start by checking to see that the queue is not empty – that is, if its first pointer points to the queue LIST struct:

```
if (temp == (LISTITEM*)queue)
```

If the queue is not empty, I execute some code (to insert the new item) and then iterate to the next item in the queue. This may look familiar. These two bits are code are identical to the code in my queue_length() function:

```
if (temp == (LISTITEM*)queue) {      // check for empty queue
    temp = NULL;
    break;
}
temp = temp->next;                   // get the next item in the queue
i = i + 1;
```

In fact, all that's different is this block of code here:

```
if (i == position) {
    item->next = temp->next;
    temp->next = item;
    item->prev = temp;
    item->next->prev = item;
    break;
}
```

This is how this works. On each turn through this loop I increment the counter variable i. The code above only executes when i equals position which is an argument passed to the function. The variable i will have the same value as position when I have iterated to the element at the desired position (the index after which I plan to add the new element).

When I arrive at that position, the code rewires all the pointers so that the new element – here that's the struct referenced by the item pointer – is inserted into the queue immediately after the item at the specified position. The item at that index is here the `struct` pointed to by `temp`.

Let's see how it does this. Here the new item's `next` pointer is set to point to the next item after the current position (`temp`) in the queue:

```
item->next = temp->next;
```

Then the `next` pointer of the item at the current position, that's `temp`, is set to point to the new item:

```
temp->next = item;
```

So if `temp` was element 3, then `item` is now placed after element 3 and before element 4. Of course, once that is done, the inserted item becomes the new element 4. The item that was previously element 4 is now element 5.

Element 3's `next` pointer now points to element 4; and element 4's `next` pointer now points to what *used to be* element 4 but is now shifted one position down the queue, so is now element 5.

OK, that's fairly straightforward. It makes sure that no links are broken in one direction – the direction that goes from element to element via the `next` pointers. To fix up the links in the reverse direction, we make exactly the same changes but this time using the `prev` pointers:

```
item->prev = temp;
item->next->prev = item;
```

The end result is that our new element is added to the existing queue and no links are broken.

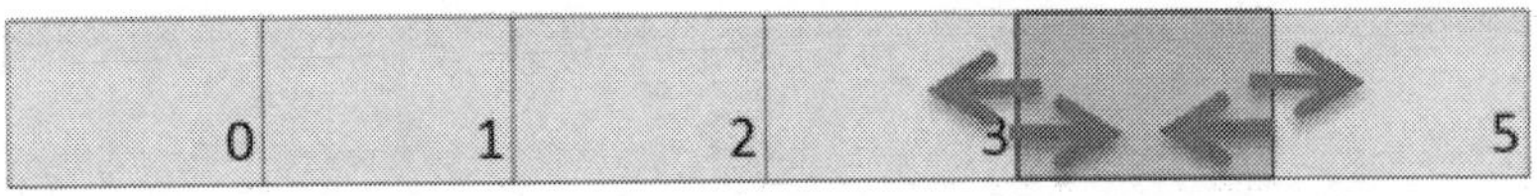

At that point we can stop iterating through the queue as there is nothing left to do and that's what the `break` does.

Incidentally, when I initialize a new list element in `main()`, I set its `data` to the *negative* of whatever index the user entered when the program was run:

```
temp->data = -requested_index;
```

There's no significance to the negative value other than to make it easy for me to see which element is the new one when I run the program.

Initially, the length of the queue is 5. It contains five elements. Let's suppose I want to add a new element after the element at index 3. The queue is indexed from 0 so the index 3 indicates the fourth element. I run the program and, when prompted, I enter 3:

```
the length of the queue is 5
enter the index of the queue entry ... 3
```

And this is the result.

```
added item at 3
the length of the queue is now 6
data: 0
data: 1
data: 2
data: 3
data: -3
data: 4
```

The queue started out with five items. Now it has six. And the new one (here containing the data `-3`) has been added *after* the element at index 3.

9 – Function Pointers

Up to now we've looked at pointers to data. It is also possible to have pointers to functions. Function pointers are typically used when handling asynchronous events – events that can happen at unpredictable moments. These events need to trigger a function call to handle them.

For example, you may want to call a certain function when an event signals that the final document in a printer queue has been printed. Or you may want to call a function when a specific mouse event occurs – say when a button or a menu item is clicked in your application.

If you've never used them before, function pointers may seem a bit obscure and it is quite possible that you may never need to use them. But in special cases they are useful and it is certainly worth knowing about them.

Function Pointer Declarations

At first sight, the syntax for declaring a function pointer may look a bit odd. Here is how I declare a pointer to a function that takes an `int` argument and returns an `int`:

```
int (*test)(int);
```

Let's see what this means:

`int`	The type (here `int`) on the left of the declaration represents the return type of the function.
`(*test)`	The name between parentheses (here `test`) is the name of the function pointer.
`(int)`	The type in parentheses (here `int`) is the type of argument that can be passed to the function.

So this pointer, `test`, can now store the address of any function that takes a single `int` argument and returns an `int` value.

You can try this out in the *FunctionPointer* project which assigns the `test` pointer to the `square()` function and then calls it in order to display the value of 4 squared:

FunctionPointer

```
#include <stdio.h>

int square(int a) {
    return a*a;
}

int main(int argc, char **argv){
    int (*test)(double);
    test = square;
    printf("Result=%d\n", test(4));
    return 0;
}
```

This is the output:

```
Result=16
```

It turns out that I can mess up the function pointer declaration and (sometimes) it will still work. If I omit the argument, for instance, it works fine – with the compiler I'm using anyway:

```
int (*test)();
```

If I enter the wrong argument and return type it still compiles:

```
double (*test)(double);
```

But when I run it, the results are not what I expect:

```
Result=0
```

In short, the syntax is tricky. Even though some incorrect declarations will compile – and the pointer will point to the correct function – an incorrect declaration won't always work as expected when you run the program. For that reason, it is common practice to `typedef` function pointers in advance.

typedef Function Pointers

Once you have written a correct typedef, you can use this type in your function pointer declarations, which is less error prone. Here I declare a type called PFI which is a pointer to a function that takes one int argument and returns an int value:

```
typedef int(*PFI)(int);
```

Now it's easy to declare a function pointer variable, like this:

```
PFI test;
```

I assign the address of a function to the test variable like this:

```
test = square;
```

Now I can use the variable name test instead of the function name:

```
test(4);
```

This works because test points to the square() function.

An Array of Function Pointers

A single piece of code can call different functions using function pointers:

FunctionPointerArray

```
typedef int(*PFI)(int);

int identity(int a) {
    return a;
}

int square(int a) {
    return a * a;
}

int cube(int a) {
    return a * a * a;
}
```

FunctionPointerArray (continued)

```
int fourth(int a) {
    return a * a * a * a;
}

PFI power[] = { identity, square, cube, fourth };

int main() {
    char input[50];
    int value;
    int exponent;
    int result;

    printf("Enter a number to select a function ... \n");
    printf("[1] identity, [2] square, [3] cube, [4] fourth\n> ");
    exponent = atoi(gets(input));
    if (exponent <= 0 || exponent > sizeof(power)/sizeof(PFI)) {
        printf("ERROR: out of range!\n");
    } else {
        printf("Enter the value\n> ");
        value = atoi(gets(input));
        result = power[exponent - 1](value);
        printf("The result is %d\n", result);
    }
    return 0;
}
```

Here I define four functions with the same arguments and return types:

`identity()`	just returns the value of the argument sent to it.
`square()`	multiplies the argument value by itself
`cube()`	multiplies it once more
`fourth()`	multiplies it yet once more.

Then I declare an array of function pointers:

```
PFI power[] = { identity, square, cube, fourth };
```

The `PFI` type is declared using `typedef` as explained earlier in this chapter. The `power` array contains the names of my four functions. These names are the equivalent of the addresses of those functions.

When the program runs I prompt the user to select a function using a number from 1 to 4. Then I ask for a value (which must be an integer) to pass to the selected function.

First I test that the integer used to select the function is valid. If it is less than or equal to zero, that's an error.

I could test if it's greater than 4 here but, who knows, maybe I will want to add more functions to my array later on so I've written this test instead:

```
if (exponent <= 0 || exponent > sizeof(power) / sizeof(PFI)) {
    printf("ERROR: out of range!\n");
}
```

This says: if `exponent` (the integer value that the user entered to select a function) is greater than the size of the `power` array divided by the size of a function pointer (`PFI`) then that's an error. In other words, it is an error if the exponent integer is bigger than the number of elements in the array of function pointers.

When I want to call a function, I call the function pointer array `power` with an index:

```
result = power[exponent - 1](value);
```

Here I subtract 1 from `value` (the number entered by the user) to allow for the fact that the array is 0-based so its first index is 0 and its last index is 3. And I pass the `value` argument, between parentheses, to the function at the selected array index.

Let's see this in action. Below you can see what happens when I run the program and enter 2 to select the `square()` function. Then I enter 3 as the value to pass, as an argument, to that function. The `square()` function multiplies the argument by itself and the result, 9, is displayed:

```
Enter a number to select a function ...
[1] identity, [2] square, [3] cube, [4] fourth
> 2
Enter the value
> 3
The result is 9
```

I run the program again but now I enter 3 to select the `cube()` function. Then I enter 5 as the value to pass to that function. The `cube()` function returns the cube of the argument (5 * 5 * 5) and the result, 125, is displayed:

```
Enter a number to select a function ...
[1] identity, [2] square, [3] cube, [4] fourth
> 3
Enter the value
> 5
The result is 125
```

So there you have it: an array of function pointers that allows you to call different functions selectively at runtime.

10 – Common Pointer Problems

Pointers are one of the major sources of error in C programs. The trouble is, a pointer can point to *anything* – even things that it has no business pointing to. It can get at areas of memory that it really shouldn't be messing about with – which can cause memory corruption, memory leaks and even catastrophic program crashes.

In this final section of this book, I'll take you through a few of the most common problems that you are likely to encounter when using pointers. These include incorrect type casts, freeing memory that has already been freed, and trying to use memory that has been freed. I'll also explain memory leaks, scoping problems and why you should never dereference a `NULL` pointer.

But first I want to explore a particularly tricky subject – deep and shallow copies: why, when you copy some data from one list to another, you need to be careful that you understand when a copy is *really* a copy. Because if you make even a very tiny mistake, your program will crash.

Deep and Shallow Copies

When I gave an example of copying one list into another list (Chapter 8), I dequeued items from one list and enqueued them onto a second list. In other words, I removed them from List 1 before adding them to List 2. Why did I do that? Why didn't I just add them onto List 2 and also leave them in List 1?

The answer is that I did it in order to avoid having to deal with one of the most common problems when copying lists. Think about two lists that contain the same elements – or rather, *pointers* to the same elements.

Any operation done to the elements pointed to from one list can have unintended side-effects on the other list. For example, I may delete an element from List 2, but List 1 knows nothing about that and will continue to try to use the element that I just deleted.

If two lists contain pointers to the same elements, or if any of the *elements* (structs) in the two lists contain pointers to some other data, then there is always a danger that when changes are made in one list, those changes may have unpredictable effects on the other list.

It is important to understand that there are two ways of making a copy of some data. The first is to create a pointer to some existing data. That is called a shallow copy. There is one item of data but two pointers to it.

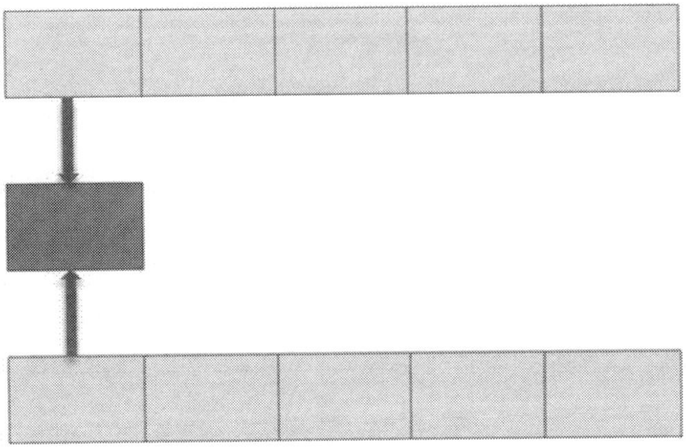

Shallow Copy

The second is to make a new copy of the data itself. That is called a deep copy.

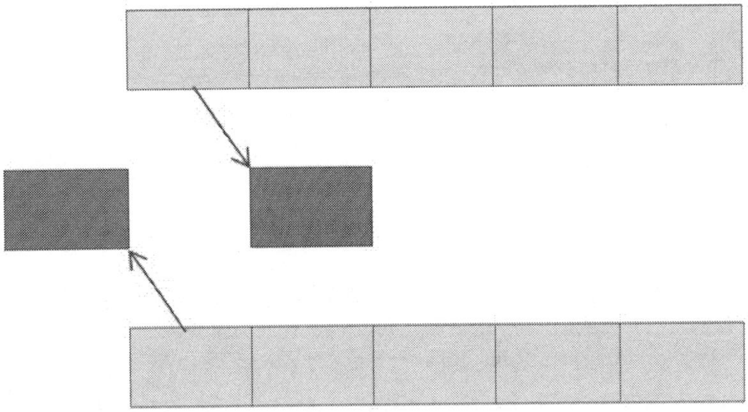

Deep Copy

Shallow copies are typically fairly fast because no real copying is done. You are just creating a new reference – a pointer whose value is the address of some existing item of data.

Deep copying is clearly going to be slower because you have to access the original data and make a copy of it at a new memory location. In my short and simple programs that may not seem like a big deal. The speed difference is negligible. But in a real-world program, the data could be enormous – you might need to make copies of enormous arrays or complex lists containing vast numbers of structs each of which contains huge amounts of data. So when making copies you need to be aware of the pros and cons of deep copying versus shallow copying.

Shallow Copies

Shallow copies are fast and efficient. They don't mess around with the original data and they don't have to make new copies of it. But they are inherently unsafe. If you make changes to one copy, those changes can affect the other copy too – and not necessarily in a good way!

Deep Copies

Deep copies are safer. They are *real* copies. When you make a deep copy you end up with two completely separate sets of data, which might be contained in arrays, lists or queues. At the outset those datasets contain the same data. Because they are identical copies. But when you make changes to one set of data those changes won't propagate through to the other set of data.

How Deep is Deep?

In fact, it may not always be obvious to you when you are creating a deep copy. In some cases, you might *think* you are creating a deep copy but you aren't. I'll explain this with an example in which it may appear at first sight that I've created a completely new copy – a deep copy – of a list, until I run the program and discover a serious problem.

List Copying Problems

In the *DeepShallowCopy* sample program I show how to make both a deep and a shallow copy of a list of structs. I'm using my *Queue* program as the basis for this.

There is quite a lot of code in this example, so I am not including the full listing in this book. As always, however, the complete code is provided in the source code archive. But, in any case, you've seen most of the code in earlier projects.

Once again, the list elements are `LISTITEM` structs with `next` and `prev` pointers. The list-manager is a `LIST struct` with `first` and `last` pointers. As in several earlier programs, this program has `enqueue()`, `dequeue()` and `queue_length()` functions.

I declare three variables which will be the `LIST` manager structs for three lists – the original list and the two copies. One will be a deep copy, the other a shallow copy:

DeepShallowCopy

```
LIST original;
LIST deep_copy;
LIST shallow_copy;
```

Let's look first at this shallow copy:

```
temp = original.first;
do {
    temp1 = (LISTITEM*)malloc(sizeof(LISTITEM));
    memcpy(temp1, temp, sizeof(LISTITEM));
    enqueue(&shallow_copy, temp1);
    temp = temp->next;
} while (temp->next != original.first);
```

This sets the `temp` pointer (a pointer to `LISTITEM`) to point to the first element in the original list, which contains a few `LISTITEM` structs:

```
temp = original.first;
```

Inside the loop, it creates some structs. Each time the loop runs, it allocates some memory for a new list item and uses `memcpy()` to copy the data from the *original* element, pointed to by `temp`, into the *new* element, pointed to by `temp1`:

```
temp1 = (LISTITEM*)malloc(sizeof(LISTITEM));
memcpy(temp1, temp, sizeof(LISTITEM));
```

It calls `enqueue()` with the address of the `shallow_copy` destination list (which is here a queue) and a pointer to the new element, `temp1`. The `enqueue()` function adds the new element to the queue. It then sets temp to the next item in the original queue so that item can be processed on the next turn through the loop:

```
enqueue(&shallow_copy, temp1);
temp = temp->next;
```

At first sight, it may seem that I must now have two distinct copies. The `memcpy()` function – and other similar functions – copy bytes from one chunk of memory to another. It makes an exact copy, so surely my `shallow_copy` queue should contain completely new copies of the original structs.

Well, let's run the program and see if that's so. And what I find is that there's good news and there's bad news. The good news is that, yes, the `shallow_copy` queue contains the correct data – it's a true copy of the original queue, I can see that here.

```
data in shallow copy queue is '0' at address 00676DC8
data in shallow copy queue is '1' at address 00675430
data in shallow copy queue is '2' at address 0067A9E0
```

The bad news is that later on in my program, after I delete the original queue (leaving – or so I had assumed – the shallow copy untouched) and then I try to iterate through the `shallow_copy` queue, I see this:

```
the length of the shallow copy queue is 3
data in shallow copy queue is '¦¦¦¦¦¦¦¦¦¦¦¦¦¦¦¦g' at address 00676DC8
data in shallow copy queue is '¦¦¦¦¦¦¦¦¦¦¦¦¦¦¦¦   ' at address 00675430
data in shallow copy queue is '¦¦¦¦¦¦¦¦¦¦¦¦¦¦¦¦¦¦0Û2wØ█' at address 0067A9E0
```

It appears to contain meaningless junk instead of the data that I thought I had copied. What's going on?

To help understand the problem, I've printed out the addresses of the data in each `struct` in the queues and also the address where that data is stored. I can see that in the shallow copy, the addresses are the same as in the original copy:

```
data in original queue is '0' at address 00676DC8
data in original queue is '1' at address 00675430
data in original queue is '2' at address 0067A9E0

data in shallow copy queue is '0' at address 00676DC8
data in shallow copy queue is '1' at address 00675430
data in shallow copy queue is '2' at address 0067A9E0
```

So when I delete the original queue and free the memory of each of its elements, the shallow copy continues pointing to the memory locations that previously stored the data that I just deleted. But now those locations contain invalid data.

To understand why that is, we need to take a close look at the `listitem struct` that defines the elements of the queue:

```
typedef struct listitem {
    struct listitem *next;
    struct listitem *prev;
    char *data;
} LISTITEM;
```

Notice that that its `data` is not a simple `int` as in my earlier examples. This time it's a pointer to `char`. That's a common data type as it's the way strings are declared in C.

Remember that the value of a pointer is a number. It's a number that indicates the address at which some data – here a `char` or a string – is stored. When I create a copy using `memcpy()`,the *value* of each pointer is copied into the structure added to the new queue.

```
memcpy(temp1, temp, sizeof(LISTITEM));
```

That means that each `data` item (that is, the `char` pointer inside each `struct`) in the `shallow_copy` queue points to *the same memory location*, as the `char` pointer in the structs in the `original` queue. That's because the *value* of each pointer in each copied `struct` is the same value, the same *address*, as the pointer in the original `struct`.

So, if the `data` pointer in Element 0 of the *source* queue (`original`) points to a string starting at address `0067DC8` (here shown in hexadecimal), then the `data` pointer in Element 0 of the *copied* queue (`shallow_copy`) also points to a string starting at address `0067DC8`.

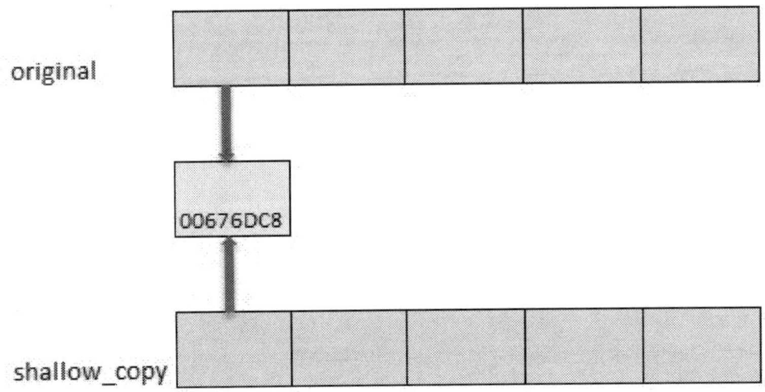

So what happens when the `original` queue is destroyed? Let's see…

```
do {
    temp = dequeue(&original);
    if (temp != NULL) {
        free(temp->data);
        free(temp);
    }
} while (temp != NULL);
```

This code frees the memory of the strings referenced by the `data` pointer in each `struct`. But the pointers in the structs in my `shallow_copy` queue *continue to point* to that memory. Which is why I end up seeing junk when I try to display the data from the shallow copy *after* the original queue was destroyed.

List Copying Solution

Let's see if we can solve this problem. This is how I create and initialize the `deep_copy` queue:

DeepShallowCopy

```
temp = original.first;
do {
    temp1 = (LISTITEM*)malloc(sizeof(LISTITEM));
    memcpy(temp1, temp, sizeof(LISTITEM));
    pdata = (char*)malloc(MAXBUFLEN);
    memcpy(pdata, temp->data, MAXBUFLEN);
    temp1->data = pdata;
    enqueue(&deep_copy, temp1);
    temp = temp->next;
} while (temp->next != original.first);
```

This code starts off in the same way as the code for creating `shallow_copy`. It copies the data using `memcpy()`. But this time there is another step. Here I use the `pdata` variable, which I declared earlier, as a pointer to `char`. I allocate a new block of memory to hold some string data. For simplicity, I'm allocating 10 bytes here, as defined by the `MAXBUFLEN` constant:

```
pdata = (char*)malloc(MAXBUFLEN);
memcpy(pdata, temp->data, MAXBUFLEN);
```

Then I make a *new copy* of the string data whose address is now referenced by `pdata`. And finally I assign the address of this *new copy* of the string to the `data` pointer of my copied `struct`:

```
temp1->data = pdata;
```

Only after this is done do I call `enqueue()` to add the copied `struct`, with its `data` pointer now pointing to a new copy of the string data:

```
enqueue(&deep_copy, temp1);
```

I can then safely delete the original queue, and free the memory used by the structs and the strings to which their `data` pointers point – because my new queue, the one that is truly a deep copy, has no pointers to any data items of any description that were referenced by the original queue.

When I run the code again, you can see that to be true:

```
after deleting the original queue ...
the length of the deep copy queue is 3
data in deep copy queue is '0' at address 0014D7A0
data in deep copy queue is '1' at address 0014D9C0
data in deep copy queue is '2' at address 0014DAD8
```

The `deep_copy` queue, and all its string data, remains intact after the original queue is destroyed. If you look at the addresses of its data items you can clearly see why that is the case.

Whereas the `data` pointers in `shallow_copy` reference strings at the same addresses as in the original queue, the `data` pointers in `deep_copy` reference *copies* of the original strings that are stored at different addresses in memory:

```
data in original queue is '0' at address 00145430
data in original queue is '1' at address 00146DB8
data in original queue is '2' at address 0014D730

data in deep copy queue is '0' at address 0014D7A0
data in deep copy queue is '1' at address 0014D9C0
data in deep copy queue is '2' at address 0014DAD8

data in shallow copy queue is '0' at address 00145430
data in shallow copy queue is '1' at address 00146DB8
data in shallow copy queue is '2' at address 0014D730
```

Bugs that result from making shallow copies can be hard to track down. In some cases, as I've shown here, you may *think* you are making deep copies when in fact the pointers in the individual elements of the copied list point to the same data as the pointers in the original list.

Incorrect Memory Allocation

Allocating the wrong amount of memory is a recipe for disaster. We've seen this problem before but it is so important that it is worth repeating: namely, when allocating memory you must make sure that you allocate the right amount. It's dangerous to assume that you know how much memory some data will require. For example, if you write a bit of code to `malloc(4)`, it will work with a 4-byte integer but it won't work with an 8-byte double.

As explained in Chapter 6, things can get even more complicated with structs due to the way that data is aligned. Change the order of fields in a `struct` and you change the amount of memory it needs.

For instance, if you've declared a type of `struct` as `MYSTRUCT` – and it contains 24 bytes of data it would be unsafe to allocate memory like this:

```
p = (MYSTRUCT*)calloc(COUNT, 24)
```

That's because the actual amount of memory needed might depend on the order of the fields in the `struct`. In some cases, you might need more than 24 bytes of memory. It is safer, therefore to use the `sizeof` operator when allocating memory like this:

```
p = (MYSTRUCT*)calloc(COUNT, sizeof(MYSTRUCT));
```

The example shown here is found in my *AddressArithmetic3* sample program. If you can't recall the details of this problem, you may want to re-read the sections in Chapter 6 all about data type alignment on boundaries.

Casting Pointers

When you cast a pointer you are not really changing anything. But an incorrect cast can cause problems. A pointer can point to anything. But when you need to access the actual data at the address to which it points you may need to cast the pointer to the correct data type. Casts are placed in parentheses, like this:

```
p = (MYSTRUCT*)calloc(COUNT, 24);
```

This casts the generic pointer returned by `calloc()` to a pointer to `MYSTRUCT`.

What is a cast?

When you cast one type to another you are not actually *changing* one type to another. What you are doing is giving an instruction to the compiler telling it that as you know that the thing you are casting will be of the type you are casting it to, so it should let you treat it as that type.

If, for example, you cast a pointer `p` to point to a specific type of `struct` and you then use that pointer to get at the fields of that structure, the compiler shouldn't treat it as an error.

Without casting the pointer `p`, the compiler doesn't know what it points to – it only knows that it is a pointer to *something*. It could be anything. Your cast tells it that it will point specifically to a `MYSTRUCT struct`. From now on, it's your responsibility to make sure that *that* is really what it points to.

The compiler assumes you know what you are doing, so you had better make sure that you do too. Remember that a cast is not something magical that *converts* one type to another type. It is an instruction to the compiler to let you treat one type as another type.

But if you now go ahead and point `p` at something that is not a `MYSTRUCT`, the compiler is not going to help you out. Your program will, in all probability, just crash. It is entirely up to you to make sure that the type you cast to is the type your code will actually use.

Incorrect Casts

Sometimes incorrect casts may not be immediately obvious. For example, look back at the *GenericPointers* sample program from Chapter 3. I must admit that when I first wrote this I got the cast completely wrong.

I declared `gp` as a generic pointer – a pointer to `void` – then I created an array of strings – pointers to `char` - called `words` and then iterated over the array, casting `gp` to a pointer to `char` at each step `(char*) gp`, like this:

```
printf("item pointed to by gp is %s\n", *(char*)gp);
gp = (char*)gp + 1;
printf("item pointed to by gp is now %s\n", *(char*)gp);
```

And this is what happened.

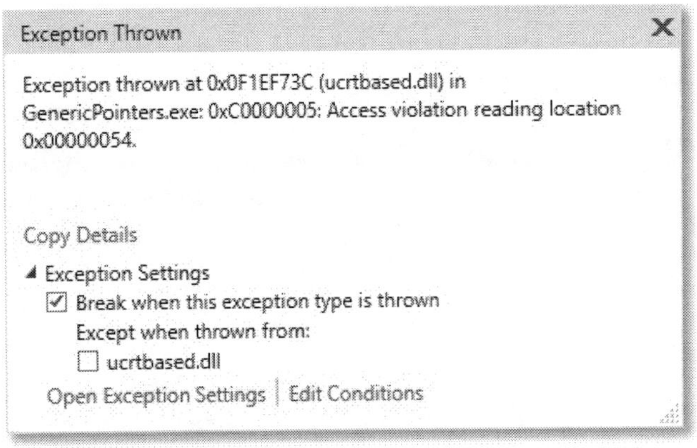

So what did I do wrong?

I forgot that my array, words, was really an array of arrays (an array containing strings which are, of course, arrays of char):

```
char *words[LENGTH];
```

So in order to dereference the arrays of chars from within the words array I needed not one star char* but two, char**, like this:

```
printf("item pointed to by gp is %s\n", *(char**)gp);
gp = (char**)gp + 1;
printf("item pointed to by gp is now %s\n", *(char**)gp);
```

So this is an example of a cast that is syntactically correct and which the C compiler didn't warn me about when I made a mistake. That's because my cast specifically tells the compiler to trust me, I know what I'm doing. But in this case, it turned out that I didn't know what I was doing. I made a mistake and the compiler didn't help me to fix it.

That is both the strength and the weakness of type casting. In this case, the compiler lets me use a generic pointer as a pointer to a specific type. If the cast is correct, that is a useful thing to be able to do. But if the cast is incorrect, the compiler won't help me out. And my program crashed.

When you cast one type to another – and especially when you cast a generic pointer to a pointer to a specific data type – you need to be very careful that the cast is correct.

Freeing Already Freed Memory

What happens if you free some memory twice? It's good to free memory when it's no longer needed so maybe it's twice as good to free it twice. Well, no, as a matter of fact it isn't. C will let you free memory referenced by a pointer variable as many times as you like but the end result won't be good. In the code shown below, you will of course notice the duplicate free() immediately. But in big programs, this sort of problem may not be anything like this easy to spot. However, the end result will be just as disastrous.

CommonProblems

```
void problem1() {
    char *b;

    b = (char*)malloc(10)
    free(b);
    free(b);
}
```

Here I allocate some memory for my `char` pointer, `b`. And then I free it twice. When I've tried running and debugging this program using both the Microsoft and Gnu C compilers and it has produced a variety of different results. If I build it for 'Release' (with no debugging) in Visual Studio, Microsoft C runs it without any obvious problem. Apart from the fact that program is supposed to print `"That's all folks!"` when it finishes.:

```
int main() {
    problem1();
    printf("That's all, folks!\n");
    return 0;
}
```

But I don't see that message. So clearly something has happened that prevents the program running that last bit of code. Then I tried out exactly the same program in the Gnu C compiler, GCC. And I saw no problem at all. Even the string `"That's all folks!"` was displayed at the end. In fact, the results of running this program can also be affected by the compiler and debugger settings you may have activated. All I can say for certain is that the effects of running this code are unpredictable.

Different compilers, different results!

This is one of the things you have to bear in mind about problems like this in C. Errors may vary according to the platform and the compiler and runtime you are using – and also the compiler settings you may have set. Sometimes an error – or a potential error – may not be obvious. Some compilers may add extra checks that make it easier to spot errors such as freeing memory twice. But errors such as this are unpredictable, which makes them harder to debug.

The fact that you don't see an error when running a buggy program in a certain compiler doesn't mean that the problem isn't there. When a problem like this occurs it may corrupt some piece of memory that doesn't cause immediate and obvious errors with one compiler but it does with another.

Even it doesn't cause a problem right away, it may cause problems later on, when some apparently unrelated bit of code is being run. Or it you may at some point decide to recompile your program using a different compiler with different build options. In either case, tracking down the bug at that stage is going to be extraordinarily difficult. So it's in your interests to spot a potential error *before* it causes trouble.

When I build and run the code that frees b twice for 'Debug' (that is, with additional debugging checks) using Visual Studio, it warns me about the problem. It throws an exception on the line where I call free() for the second time. This shows me where my error is. Once I fix it, I can be confident that the problem will not occur again, no matter which compiler I used to build my code.

What happens when you call free() twice?

When you call free() on a pointer the result is 'undefined': you are causing the memory at a certain location to be made available for storing some other data. The pointer itself, however, still points to that memory location. You don't know what that memory location is now being used for, so freeing it again can cause unpredictable ('undefined') results.

Memory Leaks

Memory leaks occur when you allocate memory but don't free that memory when it is no longer in use. That is, when it is no longer referenced in your program. You may think that potential memory leaks are easy to spot. But that isn't always the case. Look at this code. Here I want to create some strings by allocating 10 bytes for the char pointer b inside a loop:

CommonProblems

```
void problem2() {
    char *b;

    for (int i = 0; i < 10; i++) {
        b = (char*)malloc(10);
    }
    free(b);
}
```

Then I free b. That looks correct. But it isn't. I've actually lost 90 bytes of memory. That's because each time I set the b pointer to point to a new chunk of memory inside the loop I lose track of the chunk of memory that I allocated on the previous turn through the loop.

This sort of error can be frustratingly difficult to find and fix in a big program. That's because the syntax is valid and no errors or exceptions are thrown to warn me that anything is wrong. As a result, there is nothing to show that I have a memory leak.

But let's run this in the debugger. I've set a breakpoint at the end of the loop so I can watch the value of `b` in the debug window down here:

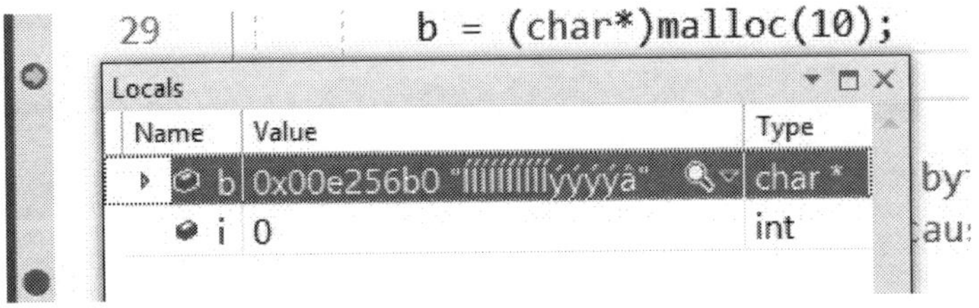

This shows the address first, then the characters at that address. The characters are random because I don't bother initializing the data here. But that's not important. It's the address that I want you to focus on. I carry on debugging until I hit the breakpoint on the second turn through the loop:

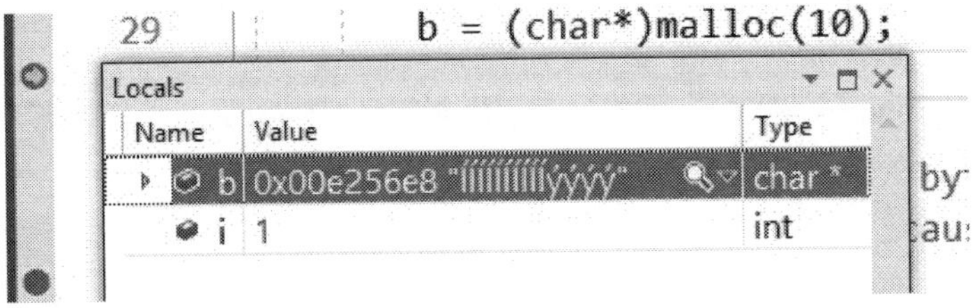

This time, memory is allocated at a different address. In fact, each time through the loop I see that memory is allocated at a different address. I carry on debugging to the last time through the loop, when `i` equals 9:

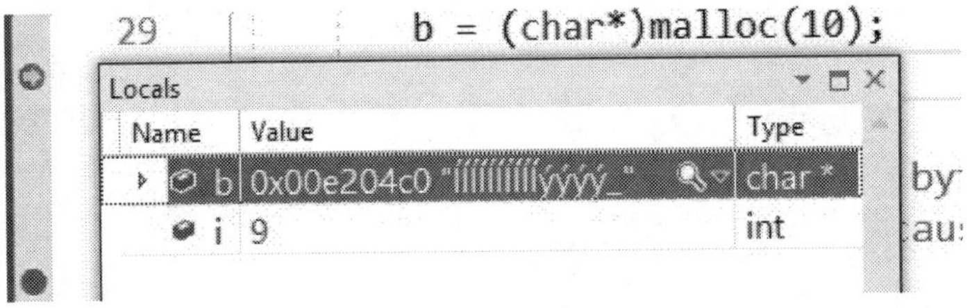

Pay close attention to this final address (which here is `0x00e204c0`). At this point the loop exits and I hit another breakpoint right at the end of the function:

When I exit the loop the address pointed to by `b` is unchanged (`0x00e204c0`). It is the address at which memory was allocated on the final turn through the loop. And it is the memory here – at this *specific* address – that is freed by this line of code:

```
free(b);
```

The memory that was allocated at all the other addresses in the previous turns through the loop – *still remains allocated.* And that's where the memory leak occurs.

Remember that even though `b` is a local variable, `malloc()` always allocates memory globally – on the heap – so that memory remains allocated even after you exit the function containing the local variable, `b`.

Using Freed Memory

Another common problem occurs when you try to use memory that has been already been freed. This is an example:

CommonProblems

```
void problem3() {
    char *b, *c;

    b = (char*)malloc(100);
    c = b;
    free(b);
    strcpy(c, "hello");
    printf("c is %s\n", c);
}
```

Here, I allocate 100 bytes for my `char` pointer `b`. I then assign `b` to `c`. Later on, I free `b`. Then I copy the string `"hello"` into the memory to which `c` points. That's a mistake.

Because that memory is no longer allocated. I freed it when I called `free()` with the `b` pointer.

So what happens when I run the code?

Once again, this is unpredictable. It may cause different problems with different compilers and it could also depend on what else you've done elsewhere in your program that might have some other side effect.

On one occasion when I ran it in Visual Studio, the program printed `"c is c"` repeatedly. But on a later occasion when I ran the same program, it ran without any (obvious) problems. It printed: `"c is hello"`. When I ran it in the CodeLite IDE using the GNU C compiler it sometimes ran without any obvious problems but sometimes it got stuck before completing.

When I debugged it in Visual Studio I could see that sometimes, even after freeing `b`, both `b` and `c` still reference a memory location containing the string `"hello"` which is why the program *seems* to work correctly. But that's just sheer luck. Those characters still happen to occupy a deallocated chunk of memory. But there is no guarantee that they will continue to do so. Here I have added some extra code to the `problem3()` function to illustrate this:

```
void problem3() {
    char *b, *c;
    char *d;

    b = (char*)malloc(100);
    c = b;
    free(b);
    d = (char*)malloc(100);

    strcpy(c, "hello");
    strcpy(d, "goodbye");
    printf("c is %s\n", c);

}
```

In principle, the memory allocated with `d` should have no effect at all on memory allocated with `b` and assigned to `c`. I am expecting c to point to the string `"hello"`. In fact, when I run this in Visual Studio, this is what I see:

```
c is goodbye
```

All I can say for sure is that trying to use memory that has been freed is not at all a good thing to do. The end results are impossible to predict, hard to debug, and are never going to be desirable.

Pointers Out of Scope

Here, I've declared an array of chars which is initialized when the user enters a name:

CommonProblems

```
char *problem4() {
    char b[20];

    printf("enter your name ... ");
    gets(b);
    return b;
}
```

I return the array and print the returned name:

```
int main() {
    printf("you typed %s\n", problem4());
    return 0;
}
```

Except it doesn't work:

```
enter your name ... Huw
you typed ¶¹ª
```

I entered `"Huw"` but it shows some mix of meaningless characters. Why? It's due to the fact that the variable `b`, is local to the function `problem4()`. It is an array, which is an address, and the return value of the function is that address.

But, as `b` is a local variable, its data is stored on the stack. Once the function exits the stack is, in effect, cleaned up. The data is not retained for later use. CodeLite with the Gnu compiler is a bit more helpful in this case. It shows me that the function returns null:

```
enter your name ... Huw
you typed (null)
```

At any rate, it doesn't matter whether you see a message showing that null was returned or, as with the Microsoft compiler, some random characters. Either way it's a bug. The variable `b` references an array whose scope is within the function and *only* within the function in which it is declared.

Even though the array, `b`, is correctly initialized and the syntax used for returning a pointer to the address of that array is correct, by the time I leave the scope of the function, the array can no longer be accessed. So the pointer returned by the `problem4()` function is not pointing to a location containing meaningful data – hence the problem.

Terminals and IDEs

If you are using an IDE with a built in Terminal emulator, you may need turn off the option to use the emulator in order to use the standard command prompt. That's because a Terminal emulator may use buffering which will prevent text appearing immediately in the Terminal when you print a string and then prompt the user to enter something. An alternative workaround is to add this line of code prior to printing and reading strings to and from the Terminal:

```
setbuf(stdout, NULL);
```

If in doubt, just load up your system prompt and run the program directly from that prompt.

Dereferencing a Null Pointer

A pointer that is set to `NULL` doesn't point to any usable memory so if I try to use that pointer I will be in deep trouble. Here's a simple example:

CommonProblems

```
void problem5() {
    char *b;
    b = (char*)malloc(10);
    b = NULL;
    b[0] = 1;
}
```

Pointer `b` is assigned `NULL`. And then I try to assign some data. Again, this may seem easy to spot in a tiny piece of code like this but it is likely to be much harder to spot in a real-world program. Let's see what happens.

When I run this program – *boom!* It instantly blows up.

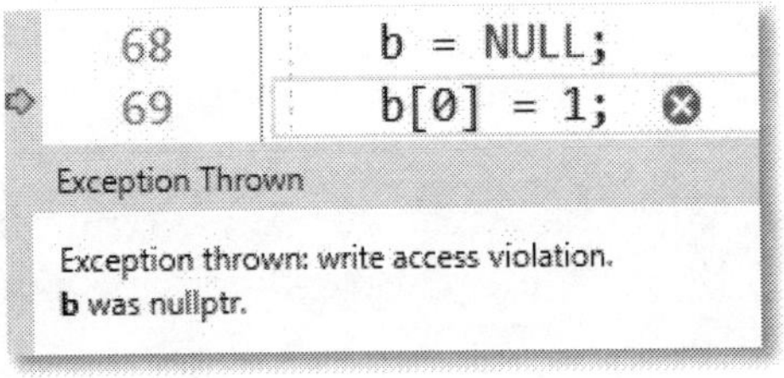

Some error of this sort should happen with just about all C compilers on desktop computers. Which is good news. Because it means that you will be able to find and fix the problem straight away.

However, if you happen to be programming microcontrollers, without any virtual memory management, the error might not be so obvious. In fact, you may never see the error at all so it will probably be extremely difficult to find and fix.

This error is sometimes called "dereferencing a null pointer". It is a serious bug and you should take great care that you never do it.

And Finally ...

You've now arrived at the end of the book. In ten chapters, we've covered a great many different topics: pointers, addresses, arrays, indirection, allocating and freeing memory, data type alignment, pointer arithmetic, linked lists, stacks, queues, function pointers, deep and shallow copying and more besides.

There are two important things to bear in mind when using pointers:

1) Pointers are, really, quite simple things. They are just variables that store numbers. The numbers represent memory locations. Pointers make it possible for us to store and retrieve data stored at those locations.

2) Pointers can be used in all sorts of very complicated ways. As I've shown in this last chapter, even simple mistakes when using pointers can result in really serious (and often, difficult-to-find) program errors.

In this book, I certainly haven't shown you *everything* you can do with pointers. For example, there are all sorts of complex data structures that you could create with pointers – branching trees, for instance, instead of linear lists. And there are numerous searching algorithms that can be used to find data items in structures linked using pointers.

The whole "point" of the *Little Book Of Pointers* is not to try to cover all the things pointers can be used for. That would make a very, very long book indeed. And probably a very boring one. In any case, there are lots of books and online tutorials about data structures, file handling, searching and sorting algorithms and so on – all of which may use pointers.

The aim of this book is to explain exactly *how* pointers work. Once you understand that, you should be able to use pointers safely in your own programs. Because you will know how to allocate and free memory, how to create linked data structures and ensure that the pointers they use always refer to – point to – the correct things.

Using pointers correctly is one of the most important skills of a C programmer. A deep understanding of pointers separates a good programmer – that is, a truly *professional* programmer – from a run-of-the-mill programmer, a hobbyist or an amateur.

Once you have studied this book carefully, you will have that skill.

It may, of course, take some time, and some coding practice, until you have really absorbed all this information – until it becomes second nature to you. To do that, take your time to re-read any topics you find especially difficult. Above all, be sure to use the source code from the downloadable archive that accompanies the book.

The best next step – to help you deepen your understanding of pointers – is to modify some of the code examples from the archive. Try rewriting them to, for example, remove not just one but an entire range of elements from a list, or to create stacks that grow downwards instead of upwards.

Once you've done that, you may want to choose your own programming subject – something that interests you. A disk utility, a simple database, a game, or whatever type of programming project you find interesting. And use pointers in that project.

There's no getting away from the fact that using pointers, and using them *well*, is difficult. But now you've completed this book, you've already gone much further to gain a really solid understanding of pointers than the vast majority of programmers. This is a skill that be of tremendous use to you. Thank you for taking the time to study this book. And good luck with your future programming!

Appendix

Using the Source Code

The source code of all the projects described in this book can be downloaded from the Bitwise Books web site:

http://www.bitwisebooks.com

The code is provided in a Zip archive and you will need to unzip the archive in order to extract the code into directories on your disk. The code is supplied as single Visual Studio Solution which, on Windows, can be loaded directly into Microsoft Visual Studio. If you haven't got a copy of Visual Studio, you can download a free copy here:

https://visualstudio.microsoft.com/vs/community/

If you are using some other C programming editor or IDE, you will need to create a project in the usual way and either load the supplied C source code files into the project or simply copy and paste the code into your main C file.

In most cases, the C code should compile without errors when using any standard C compiler on Windows, Mac or Linux. In some cases, as we have used some 'old' C functions, you may see warnings or you may need to set options to permit the use of functions which your compiler considers to be 'unsafe'. We have used these functions for reasons of compatibility (newer and 'safer' functions may not be supported by all compilers). In your own projects you would probably prefer to use whichever functions are recommended by your compiler. For the purposes of this book – understanding how pointers work – this is not an important consideration, however.

Little Books Of ...

The Little Book Of Pointers is one of a series of '*Little Books Of* …' for programmers. In each *Little Book* we aim to give you *just the stuff you really need* to get straight to the heart of the matter without all the fluff and padding.

We know that there is plenty of information online about standard code libraries, so we don't fill the pages of these books by duplicating that information. Instead, we aim to explain the really important details that you need to gain a solid understanding of each subject and start hands-on programming as quickly as possible.

Other '*Little Books Of* …' are:

The Little Book of C
A beginners guide to the C language:

- Fundamentals of C
- Variable & Types
- Operators & Tests
- Functions & Arguments
- Arrays & Strings
- User-Defined Types

The Little Book of Recursion
Understanding recursion techniques in C:

- Recursive Functions
- The Call Stack
- Stack Frames
- Stack Corruption
- Recursion & Scope
- Tree Structures
- Disk Directory Recursion

You can also download a number of useful free resources from the Bitwise Books web site:

http://www.bitwisebooks.com

Made in the USA
Monee, IL
08 November 2026

67383852R00087